Inspiration Meditation
&
Personal Wellbeing

...I feel certain we are beings who in the most open reaches of our understanding encompass all that is. We have profound capacities that enable us to take on the challenges of our day-to-day lives and discover the excitement, wonder, balance, joy, fulfilment and fundamental aliveness available to us all.

Inspiration Meditation & Personal Wellbeing

A Practical Guide to Balanced Living

Ken Mellor

New Age Books

New Delhi (India)

INSPIRATION MEDITATION
& PERSONAL WELLBEING

Published by
NEW AGE BOOKS
A-44, Naraina Industrial Area, Phase-I
New Delhi–110 028 (INDIA)
E-mail: nab@newagebooksindia.com
Website: www.newagebooksindia.com

ISBN: 978-81-7822-386-5

First Edition: Delhi, 2012

Printed and published by
RP Jain for New Age Books
A-44, Naraina Industrial Area
Phase-1, New Delhi 110 028. India

ACKNOWLEDGEMENTS

Writing this book was only possible through the contributions of many people who are too numerous to list. I thank them all for their generosity of spirit and their support.

First and foremost, I thank my wife, Elizabeth. We developed the book's contents during a 30-year period, and during the writing we had many hours of fruitful discussions. Without her involvement from the very beginning, the value of everything included would have been greatly diminished.

I am grateful also to my past and current teachers. Without them this book would not exist. They include Bob Keeley, Eric Berne, Len Tierney, Jacqui Schiff, Bob and Mary Goulding, Robin Maslen, Adam Davis, Swami Muktananda, Swami Krishna Gautam, Thakur Balak Brahmachari, Rex Finch, Stephen Karcher and Mother Meera. That each of them supported me so profoundly in my life is an ongoing source of wonder and appreciation.

Several people who read the manuscript made highly creative suggestions that led to many improvements in structure, style and content. They include David Carman, Jan Clark, Mark Davis, Zoe Edmonds, Robin Hobbes, Nicky Riddiford, Tony Smark and Martin Wells. Also, Jyotsna of New Age Books (India) was available, supportive and helpful throughout the writing and publication process.

I thank the many thousands of people who, over the years, used the approaches presented here in their own lives, including many who also taught them to others. I greatly appreciate their willingness and commitment to test ideas and practices in the hope that they would contribute to their lives. Any benefits they found were primarily to do with their efforts.

Special thanks are also due to Katrina Lehman for her masterful editing of the manuscript. Her efforts resulted in a much more highly polished book than the one I originally sent to her. Both she and her husband Nic did a wonderful job creating the presentation style of the content and the jacket design. They have been a pleasure to work with throughout.

CONTENTS

SECTION 4: ENLIVENING MEDITATIONS

SECTION 5: STARTING & PERSISTING

INTRODUCTION

Ever since I can remember, I have sought the freedom, openness and clarity that is available to us all. As a young child, I somehow had the knack of seeing into or directly knowing the core of people, situations and events. With this inner knowing, I understood, or at least believed that I did, what keeps things as they are and what allows them to change as they can. I also often delighted in finding the possible in what was thought impossible. Of course, many others delight in this too.

I very much wanted to find ways to contribute to people's lives, to experiment with the unknown, to seek freedom from limitations, to find cures for the incurable, to solve the unsolvable and, most importantly, to find enduring fulfilment.

My life became an exciting adventure that led me to know clearly that our real aliveness, fulfilment, health, completion and deep satisfaction as human beings comes primarily from within. These qualities arise from an all-embracing awareness – the Infinite – which is simultaneously the expanded consciousness or awareness that encompasses everything and what nourishes the very roots of our day-to-day lives.

From an early age, I also intuitively understood that much of what we are taught about life by our elders and peers is unnecessarily limited. Yes, we certainly need to take notice of what we are taught, but to fulfil the spiritual, cognitive, emotional, physical and worldly potential we all actually have, we need to test all such teachings and find out for ourselves if they are true.

The result of these adventures is that I feel certain we are beings who in the most open reaches of our understanding encompass all that is. We have profound capacities that enable us to take on the challenges of our day-to-day lives and discover the excitement, wonder, balance, joy, fulfilment and fundamental aliveness available to us all.

Many people perceive things similarly. They see through the distractions that somewhat obscure important realities. And in writing this book I am not presuming to offer anything better than you or they already know. In many parts of Asia, indeed, all over the world, there are numerous ancient traditions that imbue people exposed from birth to spiritually-based practices and understanding of all the dimensions of life and how they can be integrated with everyday living.

At the same time, with my background as a psychotherapist well versed in many Western human growth and development traditions, combined with my training as a meditation master, my perspectives on some areas may be different enough to be of some value. In particular, I have offered ways of integrating various dimensions of everyday living with Life, so that we can benefit from the freedom, meaning and purpose Life offers us all.

THREE PRIMARY THEMES

Inspiration, meditation and personal wellbeing, the three main themes in this book, provide a framework for presenting some of my discoveries. Whatever your background and hopes, my overall wish is that you will be inspired to use what you find here to go deeply into yourself and soar to the heights of your full potential.

My experience is that inspiration is present in everything: general inspiration that can guide and fulfil our lives, and specific inspirations related to particular events and issues.

Also, there are many practical ways of cultivating a full experience of personal wellbeing, and a collection of them is offered here for you to test and hopefully to benefit from.

In addition, a group of meditations is presented that can make their own special contributions. These can stand alone, or, like the wellbeing practices, they can be combined with everything else. In fact, when the practices in all three areas are combined, they produce a dynamic blend that I hope will reveal the wonders of your life to you and be of practical benefit.

GUIDING PRINCIPLES

Several principles guided the evolution of the practices presented, as well as my choice of what to include.

First, to be effective in life, because our hopes, needs and problems arise in the midst of everyday life, our responses also need to be down-to-earth and everyday. Second, a range of approaches is needed. No single practice deals with all aspects of living. Many different forces act on and in us, and potentially we need to respond to and deal with each of these if we are to realise our worldly aspirations and to find deep fulfilment. Third, simplicity is fundamental. No matter how complex people, situations or events may seem, we can always find simple recurring themes or patterns that can help us to understand and change things.

Finally, no book can contain all that could be of value to us in life. Nevertheless, I hope that you will discover at least some measure of assistance in what I have written.

HOW TO READ THE BOOK

To get the most out of this book, I encourage you to take your time in order to learn what it offers. The exercises, meditations, principles and guidelines included are designed to help you embed what you are reading into your everyday life in ways that best suit you. You could also read according to what attracts your attention most strongly. All the chapters stand alone enough for you to do this; and where you need more information, there are references to other relevant chapters. The frequent headings and subheadings, and the index, will also help you to find information easily.

Finally, I make repeated references to using a logbook at the end of the various exercises and meditations. Accordingly, I suggest you get a logbook or electronic organiser, or use the Notes pages at the end of this book. Keeping brief records will help you to fix the material in your memory (called 'anchoring' it), to understand it, and, when you review your records from time to time, to discover how much you have learnt. You are the only person who needs to see this logbook, so you can record whatever occurs to you in whatever way you want. Also, to make the process as easy as possible, keep your notes brief. Brevity is all you will need.

THE CONTENT

Divided into five sections, the content is presented in an ordered sequence in which earlier subjects contribute to the later ones.

Section 1 is about both inspiration and Life itself (called the 'Infinite' in the book). This section includes whatever it is that underlies, interpenetrates and enlivens all that exists, the nature of inspiration, why people are prompted to meditate, and the influence of events and everyday practices on personal wellbeing.

Section 2 contains ways to manage day-to-day activities. Each one helps to open and balance us enough for the Infinite to be experienced and known directly. These practices also contribute directly to the management of life's practical and spiritual challenges. This section includes material on goals, priorities, starting to meditate, grounding, centring, pure awareness, nutrition, rest and exercise.

Section 3 considers how to harness life energy actively during our everyday activities in a manner that makes us increasingly open to our deepest sense of self. It includes practices and information on feelings and emotions, daily cycles, resolving and releasing conflicts, and making effective decisions.

Section 4 introduces six sets of primary meditations, each capable of contributing profoundly to the awakening of consciousness and the establishment of fundamental (spiritual) fulfilment. They include breathing meditations, inner smile and body clenching, opening the heart, mantra meditation, awakening meditations, and ways to integrate meditation into daily life.

Section 5 deals with the common challenges involved in starting new endeavours and applying ourselves regularly so we achieve what is important to us. The last chapter includes guidelines for identifying good teachers, masters and mentors.

WE ARE ALREADY AT THE END

The practices in this book are effective because the union of spiritual and everyday fulfilment is already hardwired into all of us. It already exists deep inside us. We don't need to re-engineer ourselves to have it. Having said this, many of us do need to develop receptivity and openness if we are to experience or know directly the Ultimate Nature of the Infinite. 'Closer … than breathing, and nearer than hands and feet'[1], it is there for all of us and blocked only by habits of living, all of which we can change.

TEST FOR YOURSELF

All of what you will find here has been tried, tested and refined by many people in their own lives. Even so, as you explore the practices presented in the chapters that follow, I urge you to test everything for yourself. Part of living our lives responsibly involves testing everything and adapting any suggestions from others so that they fit the specifics of our own lives.

RECORDINGS OF THE MEDITATIONS

I developed several of the meditations included in this book. Recorded versions are available in CD or electronic (MP3) formats that are easily obtained from The Awakening Network Inc. You will find contact details at the end of the book.

Ken Mellor (Victoria, Australia 2011)

Section One
Inspiration

1
LIVING 'LIFE'

We begin by considering what Life is. While fundamental to everything, it is, nevertheless, a much-neglected subject in modern living. As a result, many of us are unsure what the Life is that animates all that we are and do, or how to recognise it. This is understandable given its infinite richness and that the deep recognition of Life that accompanies true awakening has to be multi-layered. For example, there is the direct experience of Life and, related to it though not the same as it, the direct knowing of Life, two processes or perceptions that are explored throughout the book.

> *One day while idly watching TV, I happened upon a motivational speaker who distinguished between knowing with the head (through rationality and reasoning) and knowing with the heart (through intuition and inspiration). 'We live in a world,' he said, 'that often puts much more trust on filtering everything we know through our rationality (he pointed to his head), than the trust we have for our intuitive or inspirational experiences (he pointed to his heart).'*
>
> *'For many of us,' he continued, 'our heads have to be convinced before we accept something as real. Unfortunately though, because heart knowing often cannot be proved through reasoning or experimentation, this limits us enormously. But our heart-centred knowing is different; it has its own truth embedded in it. We simply know it as true. Very significantly, too, what we know and understand through our hearts is fundamental to what is important in our lives, often far more so than our head-centred knowing.'*

His message was clear: We need to open ourselves to what we know in our hearts at least as much as what we know in our heads.[2] If we remain closed to either, we'll miss out on knowing and experiencing the full extent of Life in our lives.[3] And for that we need to explore the very roots of existence.

THE HEART OF LIFE

Imagine the following:

> *The Infinite is your very essence: a combined process of energising, enlivening, knowing, loving, enlightening, harmonising and understanding; it is silence, fragrance, sweetness, brilliance, peace, stillness, oneness and presence – all of this beyond imagining. When you experience or know the Infinite directly, as many people have, there is no space (up, down or across), no movement (from one place to another), no time (past, present or future), no duration (everything is now), no things exist (only the Infinite is), and there is no sense of self (world, body, me, I or I-Am). You know that normal language cannot easily express what you experience or know, as language is bound by space and time and the Infinite is not.*
>
> *When at one with the Infinite, what you experience or know is that everything in your world, including your body and all that goes with it, arises out of whatever this Infinity is. You realise this aliveness – this Life – is in everything; it is this that animates all living creatures; it is this – this presence, this energy – that underpins and is the very 'stuff' from which our daily experiences arise and are maintained. And as you have progressively lived the aliveness of the Infinite, your life has increasingly taken on its inherent qualities, an Infinity that has turned out to be 'all that is.' Your life, now fully at one with the Infinite, is beautiful, rich, balanced, peaceful, energetic...*

The Infinite is the beginning and end of everything. Throughout our history it has been called by many names, such as the Divine, God, Brahman, the Tao, and the Zero Point Field[4] of quantum physics. It can only truly be known and experienced when our hearts are open and our consciousness is released from the confines of space and time.

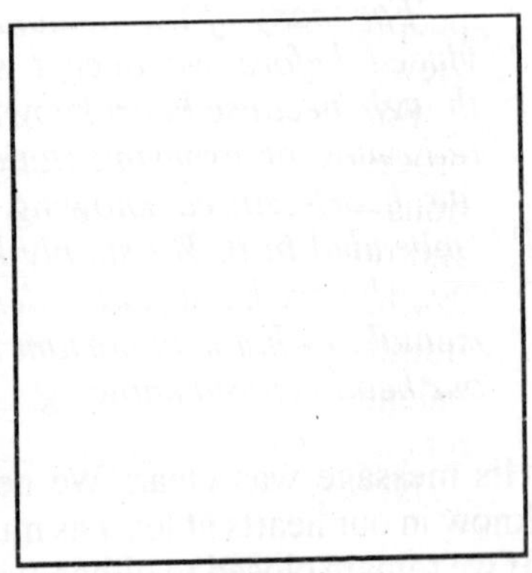

The Infinite

Exercise 1: Your Experiences of 'Infinity'. Briefly reflect on what you are experiencing after reading the above. Then log your responses, including brief descriptions of one or more of your experiences of the Infinite, even if only a small hint was present. (For example, when time seemed suspended or speeded up, or you knew something was happening although you weren't physically in the same place as the event).

Since ancient times, the main authorities on the Infinite have been great practitioners of spiritual processes, including meditation and prayer; and their efforts revealed the Infinite – the essence of Life – to many millions of people. Having extensively explored and mastered human consciousness and life processes, these people were perceived by others as having the necessary direct experience and knowing for them to be given such authority.

However, this kind of mastery is not easily realised and many millions of other people throughout this long history were unable to have the experiences and knowing of 'the greats', even after years of practice. They were unable to access these experiences because they were constrained by their perceptions of themselves, a confinement that stopped them opening up sufficiently to know the expansiveness of the Infinite.

During the last century, particularly in the 'modern rational world' of the West, many people also blocked their availability by insisting on having 'scientific' proof of the validity of the ancient claims about Life Itself and the benefits of opening up to It in their own lives.[5, 6]

Interestingly, and somewhat paradoxically, with recent advances in Western technology, things are now changing rapidly for some people previously committed to Western science. Many limited views are dissolving and old theories are being overturned.

For example, experiments show that meditation and related processes can change the structure of the brain and the way it functions – something sceptics previously thought impossible. These and other developments are helping to open the minds of people to what their hearts have long told them: that 'creation itself' is the Infinite; and that 'living processes', when welcomed by us, bring balance, health, completion and inspiration that open us to what is real and what is not real.

Now imagine this:

You are imprisoned in or tethered to a physical body that lives in a physical world (and universe). Chance events govern much of what happens: volcanoes erupt, earthquakes devastate, floods inundate, and fires scorch the earth and all living things in their paths. Your power and stature are ant-like beside these powerful forces.

You have come to accept that your body is prone to damaging diseases, injury, and accidents; that your life has a limited span; that who you are is primarily defined by what your body is capable of doing and where it lives on the Earth; that your talents have to be nurtured in order for them to grow and develop; and that you have to put ongoing effort into securing and maintaining physical, emotional and mental health.

In what you are imagining, you have all-too-brief glimpses of 'aliveness', of something much 'bigger' than you – of something that surrounds and completely saturates and enlivens you. Much as you may cherish these moments or their memories, they mainly come at unexpected times: when you are deeply touched by the natural world, at the birth of a child, when in love, when suddenly rewarded with the fulfilment of long-held dreams, or when with people as they leave this life.

At these times, it seems as if a veil between your usual 'everyday awareness' and your expansive aliveness evaporates, as if your 'world-bound-ness' is lifted into or dissolved by something much bigger than you are. This 'something' carries with it deep knowing, acceptance, understanding, unity, peace, love ... 'something' that melts away, at least for a time, your previous narrowness and inhibitions. Often at these times you think, 'I wish I could experience this all the time', and wonder, 'How can I do that?'

Exercise 2: Bodily Limitations and Inhibitions. Note in your logbook some of the limitations you notice in your bodily life as a person bound in space and time, and some experiences that seem to have lifted you out of them, even if only momentarily.

In the life just imagined, our aliveness seems to trickle through us, often barely holding its ground against all that it has to contend with. We generally don't experience an abundance of vitality or resilience, tiring quickly and feeling tired but forcing ourselves to keep going no matter what. Of course, many people don't experience struggling to quite such an extent and maybe you are one of these people. Having learnt to live a relatively balanced life, you may have an easier time. Even so, compared with what is possible, many people are still living in far more confined and limiting ways than are actually necessary or desirable.

Finally, imagine this:

You now know enough in your heart about the Infinite foundation of Life to realise that welcoming, embracing and expressing its abundance in life leads to real fulfilment. You have also found that direct knowing and inspiration come with this ongoing availability to the Infinite. You have come to understand how seemingly small practical acts have helped to transform you so that each day you are expressing Infinite Life more and more directly. Initially, you could not see how some of these seemingly insignificant approaches could make a difference, but perseverance revealed their power and value.

Every step you have taken to become both at one with and a channel for the life force available in the Infinite has been rewarded with unimagined benefits. Step by step, you have learnt to live expressively, to clarify what you see, to harmonise and create oneness in yourself and your relationships, to build your physical, emotional and mental vitality so you are fuelled more by a worldly expression of the Infinite's vitality in your everyday life, and you have increasingly digested the unfinished business from your past.

Your life is easier, carried along effortlessly in the stream of Life. You have looked for and found ways of claiming and enacting the Infinite, which you have discovered is forever seeking to transform you into Itself so you know It directly. All of this enables you to live Life fully in the world.

Exercise 3: Progressing in Living. Note briefly in your logbook what you have done that has expanded your direct knowledge or experience of the Infinite. Also, note what you have changed (knowingly or not) that enabled you to live the stream of Life more fully so you have evolved more towards living an integrated expression of the Life of the Infinite. Also note what you would still like to change.

2
Opening to Inspiration

My wife, Elizabeth, woke up in the middle of the night less than a month after the catastrophic bushfires of 2009. They had devastated the countryside near where we lived in Australia and killed 173 people. Having been trapped in our home for 13 hours in the midst of a bushfire in 2002, this latest event reawakened many unresolved feelings that she still carried.

Elizabeth felt compelled to get up immediately and start writing. And during the next six weeks she kept writing, always guided by her inner prompting.

It was an uplifting story about a family having to fight to survive a horrific bushfire, to deal with their grief over lost friends, and gradually to recover in the years that followed.

This book had a life of its own. Elizabeth did not know what would happen next as she wrote, and was often surprised at what was flowing from her into her computer. *Bushfire* became an "award-winning" book, offering soothing and resolution to traumatised adults and children.

It is an exquisite example of inspiration: an integration of Elizabeth's life experience, her concern for children and families, her social work and psychotherapy backgrounds, and her highly developed ability as an author. And it all just seemed to happen.

The whole writing process involved one flooding inspiration after another. It was a lightning strike of understanding accompanied by the profound feeling and knowing that she had to write this story. It clearly came from the Infinite and, because she was open and aligned to that, Elizabeth was able to deliver the story with all its wonderful power, complexity, simplicity and nuances.

WHEN LIGHTNING STRIKES

In 'lightning-strike' inspiration, there is a flooding of new awareness, fresh comprehension and a commitment to do something to express what is newly understood. Not always as remarkable as Elizabeth's example, inspiration can be much milder or slower, maybe even going almost unnoticed, like a vague new thought that disappears from our awareness as quickly as it arises. Of course, it can also be amazing. Whatever its impact – from profound to mild – this kind of inspiration often seems to come out of nowhere, and in a way it does.

Inspiration arises out of the 'nowhere' and 'no-when' of the Infinite. It is a direct knowing or experiencing that we inspire or 'breathe into' our everyday consciousness. It arises for us when, as physical creatures, we have (unconsciously or consciously) made ourselves receptive to the Infinite.

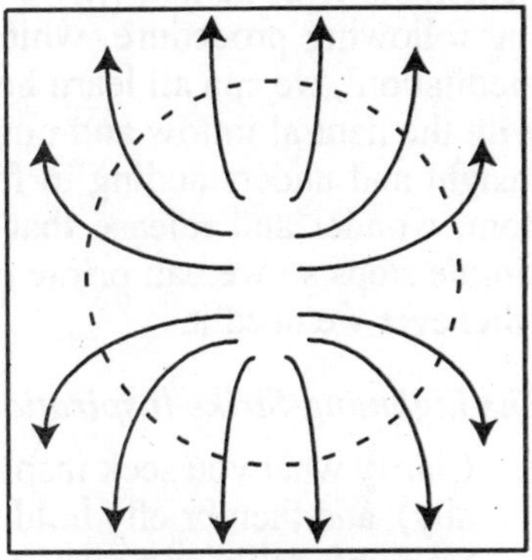

Inspiration from the Infinite

When *unconscious* of the process, we simply experience our new understanding or insight arising in us without any awareness of what is involved. This often makes unconscious inspiration seem mysterious, maybe even haphazard. By contrast, when we become *conscious* or aware of inspirational processes at work, it is fairly easy to start knowingly to use them as procedures. Many practices in this book, particularly the various forms of meditation, can help us to develop this openness and availability (see Chapters 9 to 12 and 25 to 30).

Lightning-strike inspiration can take many forms. For example, inspirations might be scientific (Sir Isaac Newton's discovery of gravity), cognitive (the solving of a long-standing mathematical or intellectual puzzle), practical (a different way of doing a household chore), spectacular (the significant inspirations that led to the development of the computer), everyday (having random ingredients and making a wonderful meal), and commercial (creating a new marketing strategy).

Most importantly, everyone is capable of having great and life-changing or everyday inspirations.

Exercise 1: Lightning-Strike Inspiration. Think back and recall any moments or periods when you experienced lightning-strike inspirations. Make brief notes of what they were, the new understanding they brought to you, and what, if anything, you did differently as a result of them.

CULTIVATING LIGHTNING STRIKES

We all have the potential to cultivate or to find inspiration deliberately. We can do this in relation to specific issues or in order to benefit our lives generally. We don't need to wait passively. Using the following procedure, which is based on an ancient form of meditation[7], we can all learn how to do this. We can learn to align with the natural inflow and outflow of awakening, and to breathe insight and understanding in from the Infinite. Imagine the freedom, wonder and release that could come from mastering four simple steps so we can prime ourselves to experience inspiration whenever we need it.

The Lightning-Strike Inspirational Procedure:

1. Clarify what you seek inspiration about (specifically or generally), and then briefly hold this in your awareness.
2. Sit comfortably and relax as deeply as you can, seeking alignment with the Infinite (see Chapters 11 to 12, and 16).
3. Whatever you experience, simply observe this and let it unfold naturally at its own pace.
4. Allow your gradual return to normal consciousness as this occurs naturally, record any insights or inspirations in your logbook, and do something minor to express them (see Evolving Decisions in Chapter 24).

You can keep repeating the four steps until you have the inspiration and understanding you are seeking. It is a good idea to allow time between repetitions – anywhere from hours to weeks. Keeping records in your logbook usually helps.

The following hints for handling each of the steps can make your learning easier:

Step 1: Keep things simple. Formulate a short phrase or sentence; for example, 'solve the problem with …', 'the best way to contact …', 'how to learn …', or more generally, 'to experience the Infinite directly.' Avoid thinking deeply about these 'seed thoughts'. Analytical thinking often blocks access to Infinite understanding. Also, logging your phrase in your book can help to anchor it so you feel relaxed about seeming to forget it in the middle of the procedure.

Step 2: Let go of the 'seed thoughts' and relax deeply or meditate peacefully. Until you can do this easily and spontaneously, you can use a *Relaxation Meditation* recording.[8] Have this ready to start so you don't have to set it up in the middle of this step. Remember to sit upright so you stay alert as you relax. Avoid making notes during this step and the next.

Step 3: Infinite experience and knowing is timeless. Open yourself to this timelessness. Avoid thinking about your issue; simply float with it. Allow enough time so the process can unfold naturally. There will be a natural end to it, although it may occasionally seem never-ending. Ride with this quality and avoid trying to force an outcome. Use awareness of what is supporting your body to help you to deal with any internal busyness.

Step 4: Your inspiration or understanding may be immediate or it may take longer. Insights from the Infinite can take minutes, hours, days or more to arrive. Remember, you are breathing in the understanding from beyond everyday experience. It is best to wait patiently, without trying to discover what your inspirations are. Relaxed readiness seems to work best. The more tension we generate during this step, the more we interfere in the process. You can use grounding and centring to help you to manage your responses and to retain your equanimity (see Chapters 9 to 12). The guidelines for Evolving Decisions (see Chapter 24) can help here too.

Exercise 2: Encouraging Lightning-Strike Inspiration. Take something small that you would like help to understand or resolve. Seek inspiration using the four steps outlined. Log what occurs.

OTHERS CAN INSPIRE US

The examples set for us by others are often very significant.

> *I now live on a rural property in south-eastern Australia. Having come from a city only a few years ago, there are many things I am still to learn.*
>
> *When we moved here, a long drought was in progress and the ground was rock-hard. Years later, the drought broke and we had months of heavy rain. Unbeknown to me, the rain turned the ground in some areas into a muddy jelly incapable of supporting any weight. When driving over one of these areas, it took less than two seconds for the left rear wheel of my tractor to sink a metre into the ground, bogging it to the axle.*
>
> *Two people offered to help pull the tractor out. The first was*

completely unsuccessful. Together, we tried to drag it out backwards the way I had gone in. The tractor hadn't moved a centimetre (an inch) after thirty minutes of hard work.

The second person arrived, looked at the way the tractor was caught, assessed the surrounding ground (he didn't want to get bogged too), and attached a cable to the front of the tractor. He pulled me out of the bog forwards in less than fifteen seconds. Here was a master at work.

I love watching masterful people. I am inspired by their capacity to assess a situation, task or problem, and to know what to do to take care of things. There is obvious finesse in what they do. They work economically, wasting little effort. Also, seeing what is required at the end, they work systematically and effectively from the existing situation to the outcome they want; and they know how to anticipate difficulties and avoid them or prevent them before they occur.

These people inspire me to master all that I do, to develop the same level of accomplishment as they demonstrate, to fill the many gaps in what I know. They give me an expanded view of myself that in itself is enough to encourage me to realise the same mastery in my own life. And, to that end, I deliberately recall masters who have inspired me to do better: a wonderful plumber, various teachers, a computer expert in his early 20s, well-known businesspeople, talented actors, Nelson Mandela, several great healers, highly trained sports people, and many more. It is their prowess that particularly inspires me.

Exercise 3: Inspiring Models You Have Emulated. Remember three people you have copied because of who they were, how they acted, and what they thought, believed or felt. What inspired you about them? Also, think about others you now admire. Remember to make notes of both groups in your logbook.

ACTIVELY SEEKING INSPIRATION

Exercise 4: Seeking Inspiration. Consider an area of your life where you would like to be doing more. Log this, and then set out on a deliberate search for people who seem to have succeeded better than you in this area. Many options are open to you: the Internet; good books, particularly ones describing people who could inspire you; and asking others if they know people who could help you. Relax as you do this, searching a little at a time is effective; after only a few weeks; even five minutes a day can make a big difference. Record the results you get in your logbook.

HOW INSPIRATION WORKS

As mentioned, inspiration comes from the Infinite. Sometimes subtly, sometimes obviously, it arises in our awareness in many forms: for example, as a new idea, thought or feeling; as a new way of seeing something old; as an underlying theme that draws together many fragments that have previously preoccupied us; as something completely new; as a significant change to something well established; or as an impulse or desire to take action.

Inspiration often touches our awareness with new light, new themes, and new feelings related to some area, interest, need, or problem in our lives. Part of what makes things inspirational is the way these breakthroughs embrace and digest our current awareness, and how they also fulfil this awareness with the new scope or dimensions that they introduce to our understanding. We are left changed, because our inspirations somehow make us more than we were. Also, our new insights reorganise our approaches to things in ways that often include a need to take action, and they produce a natural commitment in us to do so.

Inspiration can fill us with hope for the future, give us a sense of direction through hard times, awaken our creativity and, very importantly, open us to the immense resources available in the Infinite so the difficult becomes easy, the routine become exciting, the apathetic becomes committed, and the 'impossible' becomes possible. And, we can start right now.

3
REASONS FOR MEDITATING

'I've been ill for a long time and I've tried everything without success. My doctor suggested meditation might help.'

'I never seem able to relax, don't have any spare time and always have so much to do. Then, when I do get time, I can't let go.'

'Everything in my life is good. I have a lovely family and a good job. But I'm not happy and don't get pleasure from anything I do.'

'Ever since I can remember, I've felt incomplete. It's as if there's something inside me trying to get out. If only I could reach it, I'd discover my purpose for being alive.'

'I have a passionate desire to awaken spiritually and I need guidance to ensure what I'm doing will work.'

During the thousands of years of its history, people have used meditation in virtually every area of life. This has bequeathed great riches to us in the modern world. Accordingly, the four general areas I have selected for this chapter are a tiny sample of what is available. These days, many people meditate to:

- improve health.
- deal with life's pressures.
- make life enjoyable.
- promote spiritual awakening.

Exercise 1: Your Interest in Meditation. Briefly record what interests you about meditation and what you hope it will offer you. You could include any of the above reasons, or something else.

IMPROVING HEALTH

Particularly in Asia, with its ancient traditions in health promotion and healing, people have long known of the extraordinary contributions meditation can make to health. By contrast, people in the West have relied more on technological interventions and have only started to realise the power of meditation relatively recently. This is partly because of the experiences of the many people who now meditate there and partly from the increasing number of informative research projects that validate, in Western terms, the wonderful results known elsewhere for millennia.

Both Eastern and Western sources of information are now increasingly regarded as valid, and for those who favour Western-style scientific proof, consider the following examples[9, 10, 11].

- Clear evidence that some illnesses have been cured or ameliorated using meditation; that the progression of illness can be slowed or stopped; and that recovery from accidents or illness (such as cancer, heart disease, strokes, and infections from viruses and bacteria) can be accelerated.
- People who meditate on a daily basis tend to live longer, have fewer accidents and less illness, and recover from physical problems faster.
- Advanced meditators can produce changes in their bodily processes, feelings and thoughts, simply by meditating in specific ways.
- Concentration, persistence, equanimity and personal balance are all encouraged to a high degree by meditation.
- Meditative practices have rejuvenating effects: some long-term meditators have organ systems with functional ages of twelve or more years less than their actual ages.
- MRI images show distinctive alterations in brain structure and processing amongst advanced meditators, indicating that meditation promotes positive physical changes.

There are many specific meditations for promoting general health and healing after illnesses or accidents. The *Complete Health Meditation* is an example of one that promotes both.[12]

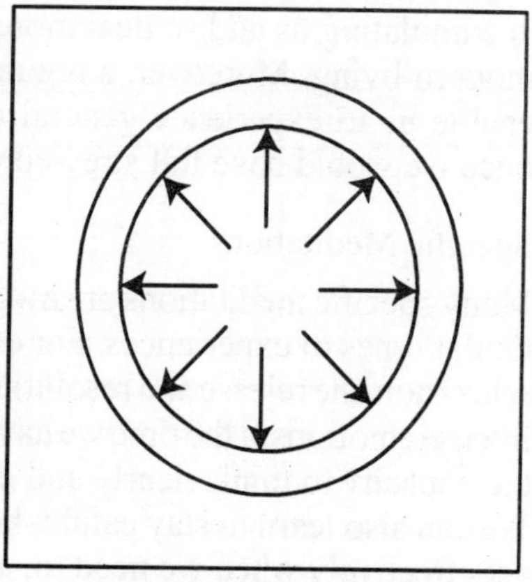

Building Life Force in the Body from the Infinite

There are also powerful meditations that help us to intensify and build up the life force or life-energy (variously called names like prana, chi or shakti) in our bodies, energy that is especially available to us as we hold our bodies in our awareness while we align with the Infinite. This energy promotes both healing and general aliveness. Many meditative physical practices (including hatha yoga, qigong, tai chi and kum nye) and mantra meditations (e.g., the *Vedic Mantra Meditation*[13] introduced in Chapter 29) are also effective for doing this.

DEALING WITH LIFE'S PRESSURES

Modern living is very stimulating. The pace of life is accelerating more and more rapidly. The urban environments in which many people live are saturated with sound, movement, visual intensity, tastes and smells (some soothing and some disturbing), as well as toxic chemicals that pollute our food, air and water, and disturb the natural balance in our bodies. This stimulation perpetually bathes and, at times, assails us. Just looking around the average shopping area or busy street scene and feeling the impact on us can easily convince us of this.

In addition, the routine use of computers has promoted even more intense pressure on children at school, parents at home, and people in the workforce. They are expected, and expect themselves, to live like computers – always on and never off – using high-level multi-tasking capacities 24/7. The damage this is doing to personal wellbeing in adults and the forming consciousness of children is becoming increasingly obvious.

Fortunately, meditation can be of great help. For example, many specific ways of meditating require that we stop physically, even if only briefly, and this helps us to slow down internally.

Meditation can also help us to respond differently to whatever is stimulating us and so deal more effectively with the stresses of modern living. Moreover, a regular daily meditation practice can enable us to experience general equanimity and balance, where once we would have felt stressed or distressed.

Specific Meditations

Many specific meditations are available to help us to deal with particular types of experiences. For example, meditation can promote relaxation, the release and resolution of feelings, the management of intense emotions at the time we have them, release from anxiety, and the capacity to think clearly and effectively while under pressure. We can also learn to stay calm when challenged uncomfortably, to act effectively when we need to, and to withhold action when that would be better. The Grounding Meditation[14] and the Relaxation

Meditation[15] are very effective for promoting these types of responses (see Chapters 9, 10 and 16).

Regular Daily Practice

The types of meditations just mentioned are often used on an event-by-event basis as situations arise: something occurs and we meditate to manage our responses to it. If we continue to use meditations like this, we can experience both the specific benefits at the time and a generalised improvement in our abilities to cope with situations that we used to find troublesome.

We can also do more, for by meditating every day, we promote deep change in the foundations of our bodily lives. Our inner processes (sometimes called 'core processes') become clear and refined, which produces continuing ease and balance within us. We increasingly remain calm and tranquil, even in the midst of mayhem. Like being in the eye of a cyclone, we can be surrounded by intense activities and events, yet remain balanced, clear and harmonious. The results are twofold. Because our day-to-day turbulence is subsiding, we experience a great increase in personal wellbeing. We also become increasingly open to the Infinite and more available to our life force.

As well as the *Grounding Meditation* and the *Relaxation Meditation*, The *Vedic Mantra Meditation* (see Chapter 29) and the *Awakening Meditation* (see Chapter 30) are especially powerful ways to produce these profound changes. Many other meditations are also available in other approaches.

MAKING LIFE ENJOYABLE

The results of meditation can reach into every aspect of our lives. It can help us to make the most of what we have and to discover more ways to experience satisfaction and enjoyment.

Many people develop better self-esteem. They also become more tolerant of others, and much warmer and closer to others. They develop more clarity about and respect for people, work with greater commitment, cooperation and focus, find their family lives more fulfilling, and have greater satisfaction in their intimate relationships. These and other wonderful changes usually accompany the inner transformations that meditation helps people to make, transformations that are obvious in how happy, contented and at ease many of them become. The expression 'the peace … that surpasses all understanding'[16] describes this beautifully.

PROMOTING SPIRITUAL AWAKENING

Vast numbers of people meditate to develop their spirituality in some way. They do it to experience the deeper reaches of who they are, to expand their consciousness, to embrace the Infinite and to participate in the wonders that are available in the spiritual dimensions of their beings.

These people often either already know or sense that fundamental nourishment comes from the Infinite and from nowhere else. In other words, they meditate as a way of feeding themselves with what some call divine energy or divine consciousness.

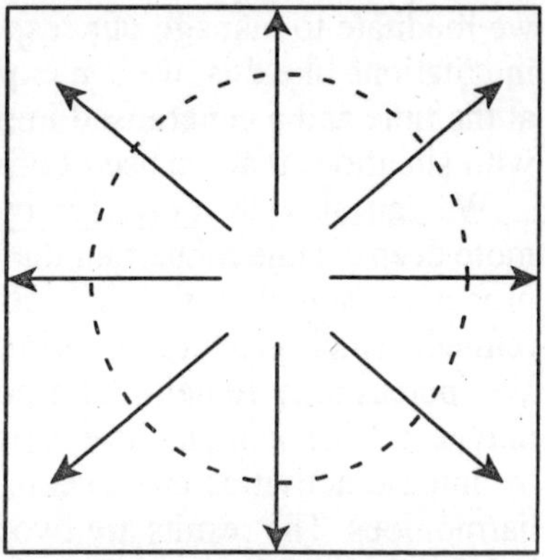

Nourishment from the Infinite

In the early days of our practice, this is often experienced (seen, heard or felt) as energy streaming through us, saturating our bodies, thoughts and feelings as it does.

While seemingly mythical to some, many millions of people in the past have discovered these results; and millions of others are doing so today. They seek the sustenance, expansion, fulfilment, wonder and transcendence that come from the long-term practice of meditations that are designed to encourage spiritual awakening. And you could do this, too, if you are interested. Of course, there is the challenge of needing to persist for long enough to experience these results, something we all face.

The effects are truly extraordinary: to be able to make an internal shift at will that enables us to feel flooded with lovely feelings, to find inspiration in our lives, to perceive clearly and confidently, to understand the situations we are in, and to feel reassured that the directions of our lives are right for us. More importantly for many, we can also discover that our so-called 'selves' dissolve into the apparent nothingness of the Infinite from which all-knowing, experience and existence arises (see the *Awakening Meditation* in Chapter 30.)

Exercise 2: Meditation and Changing Your Life. Take a few moments to consider your reasons for reading this book. Then, thinking about meditation, ask, 'What do I want to change in my life? Is it my health, how I deal with stress, my enjoyment of life, my spiritual openness and availability, or something else altogether?' Log your answer in your book.

4
REALISING PERSONAL WELLBEING

When we have wellbeing, we are physically, emotionally, mentally and spiritually in balance; we experience day-to-day satisfaction and fulfilment; we have inner direction and an impression of being guided that comes from having an overall purpose in our lives; and we have a sense that we are encompassed by a reality much larger than ourselves, a benign reality that offers completion, awakening and fulfilment.

This reality is known as I-Am and is the aspect of our everyday consciousness that participates in the Infinite as much as is possible for us.

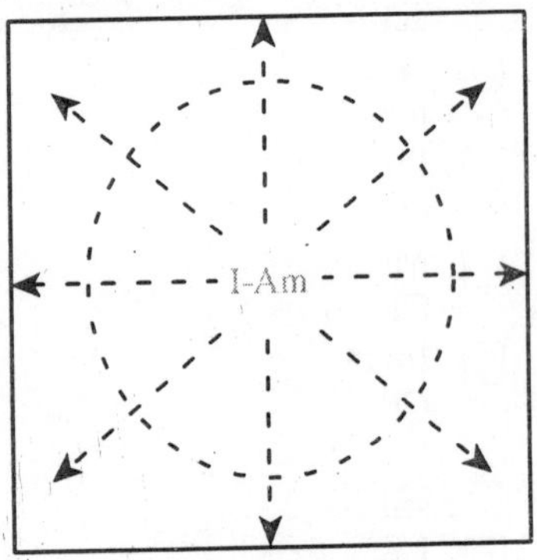

I-Am as the Infinite's Entryway into Everyday Life

With personal wellbeing, we also experience wholeness, vitality and aliveness. We have a sense of our place in the world. At the same time, we have overall confidence that we can cope with life's demands and, if necessary, we can ask others for help.

I remember someone who was a particularly good example of this. He had a physical, emotional and mental vitality about him that was obvious. He was at home within himself; and he was present with and available to others. He had a steadiness about him that seemed to arise because of his natural physicality, as if 'his feet were planted in the ground' and all other aspects of him had taken on a related balance.

He lived very much in the present, not getting caught up in past injustices nor dwelling on anxious fantasies about the future. He was alert and responsive to what was going on around him. He could deal with life because he was in an ongoing state of availability to what he faced day by day. And all of this was supported by his commitment to a spiritual view that he used to guide, manage, balance and live his life.

DEVELOPING WELLBEING

In my own and other people's experiences, the practices in this book can contribute significantly to our wellbeing.

Exercise 1: Assessing Your Wellbeing. In this exercise, we are considering what we can do deliberately to secure our personal wellbeing. Tick/check the boxes below to indicate activities you already use to take care of yourself and to promote your wellbeing. Add others if your practices are not here. Do you:

- ☐ Cultivate awareness of the life force in you and everything else (live Infinite aliveness)? (See Chapters 1 and 25.)
- ☐ Have a sense of purpose that guides your interests and activities (use goal-setting)? (See Chapters 5 to 7.)
- ☐ Nourish your body (eat and drink) what it needs? (See Chapters 14 and 15.)
- ☐ Promote bodily strength, resilience and health (rest and exercise)? (See Chapters 16 and 17.)
- ☐ Maintain emotional and mental balance (use grounding)? (See Chapters 9 and 10.)
- ☐ Imagine and ensure your success (use creative release)? (See Chapters 5 to 6 and 33.)
- ☐ Cultivate a sense of self as a physical, emotional, thinking, spiritual being (use centring)? (See Chapters 11 to 12.)
- ☐ Live in alignment with your basic rhythms (live cyclically)? (See Chapters 20 and 21.)
- ☐ Make effective decisions (make deliberate decisions)? (See Chapter 24.)
- ☐ Cultivate love, tenderness, cherishing and oneness with others (open your heart)? (See Chapters 28 and 31.)
- ☐ Develop awareness of your inner self, your 'I-Am' (meditate)? (See Chapters 11 and 12, and 30.)
- ☐ Promote everyday happiness and spiritual fulfilment (contribute to the Earth and those around you)?

As you will find in the chapters that follow, most of these areas are discussed directly, and simple, practical ways of gaining the available benefits in them are presented.

PERSISTING IN WHAT WORKS

For you to get these benefits, the only requirement is your persistence, including persisting through the 'normalising process'.

Most of us want to experience personal wellbeing and celebrating when we have it is an excellent practice because it encourages us to persist in seeking what we want in our lives. This may seem obvious: something works, so keep doing it in order to keep getting the benefits. Paradoxically, however, not everyone continues to celebrate when things are going well.

A clue to understanding this paradox is in the way we stop noticing on-going experiences. All of us tend to do this. When we've had an experience for long enough, we no longer know it is there. The following examples demonstrate how quickly our senses adjust:

- Shortly after emerging from a dark place, the sun quickly stops seeming so bright.
- We stop noticing regular noises near where we live.
- In summer, we don't notice moderately hot temperatures.
- Only a short time after smelling something strong when we enter a room, we stop smelling it.

This normalising process relates to everything – both what we like and enjoy, and what we don't like. For example, when we experience ongoing happiness, peace, vitality or pleasure, or ongoing disturbance, hunger, pain or conflict, their intensity gradually diminishes so we notice them less or they disappear.

This can lead to problems. For example, when our ease and pleasure diminish because our systems have normalised them, we no longer get direct reinforcement for continuing to do what produced the results that previously left us feeling good.

Similarly, when we experience less pain or discomfort because our systems have normalised them, we are prompted less to remember how we once wanted to deal with them.

These two reactions can partly explain why people stop doing what helps them to feel more comfortable and fulfilled in life, even when they know what works; and partly explains why people will stay on in unhappy or unhealthy situations. We simply stop noticing the full intensity of what we are experiencing and so don't have the same level of motivation to continue doing what is good for us. (See Section 5: Starting and Persisting.)

Exercise 2: Effective Action that We Stop Taking. Make a brief record in your logbook about each of the following:

- Three things you have done that helped you to feel better, to solve problems or to clear obstacles from your path.

- Three things like this first list that initially helped, but that you stopped doing after a while (maybe the same ones).
- Any connection between stopping what you used to do and getting used to what you were experiencing.
- How the reduction of intensity may have reduced your motivation to keep actively promoting your wellbeing.

Section Two
PRACTICES FOR A NEW LIFE

5
Getting Organised Using Goals

'I'm in big trouble.' The young man talking to me was looking harried. 'I'm so disorganised. I start to do one thing and before I've finished it, I start doing something else. Then I do a third and a fourth ... I can spend a whole day jumping from one thing to another like this and end up not completing anything. I'm going to lose my job if I don't change.'

'Is there more?' I asked.

'Well, yes. The other day, the boss asked me for my weekly report and I had to tell him I'd completely forgotten it. I was so busy jumping from one thing to another, I'd lost track.'

He was obviously distraught, so I nodded encouragingly and he continued. 'Every time the phone rings, I get focussed on that; then someone comes to my work station and I get engrossed in what he wants...'

As he fell silent, I knew he was talking about a chronic process and said, 'So, basically, you're easily distracted and you let every interruption determine what you do and when you do it.'

'Yes, that's right,' he replied. 'I get lost in it all; and I guess I have to say my whole life is like that.'

A sense of direction is important, both specifically in our everyday activities and generally in our lives. When we have clear goals, purposes or visions guiding what we do, everything can be balanced in relation to them. We can be systematic, assess the outcomes of our efforts, and act reliably with others. Just as significantly, we can more easily remain aware of how fulfilled we are in our lives as a whole.

This young man's story also illustrates that without specified goals to guide us we can get into all sorts of difficulties. We can experience ourselves as drifting, allow things to slip that need our attention, have little awareness of how successful we are (even with trivial things), and be disorganised and unreliable.

Exercise 1: How Organised Are You? Briefly record your answers to the following questions in your logbook:

- Are you well organised or disorganised in your life?
- Do you manage your life or does it manage you?
- Do you mostly drift or react your way through your day?
- Are you selective about what you do and when you do it?
- Are you proactive in completing the tasks that are your responsibility?

GOALS

Definition: A goal is an end result.[17] It is the situation or state of affairs that will exist when we have completed what we have set out to do.

Clearly, many things can become goals. Whenever something does not exist, is not available or has not yet been reached, deciding to create it, to make it available or to reach it turns that something into a goal.

Goals are central to completing what we set out to do. In fact, to thrive in life and accomplish what we have set ourselves, we all need to know what our goals are and how to be clear about them; we also need to follow through on what we have decided to do.

Accordingly, taking time to be clear on our goals – the first step – is not a distraction, as many people in difficulties with routine or bigger tasks often think. Far from it, defining our goals clearly is fundamental to achieving anything systematically, including what we need to do to secure our personal wellbeing.

Principle 1: Systematically setting goals is one of the simplest ways of becoming well organised and living purposefully.
The moment we start to become goal-directed in our lives, we can discover a sense of clarity and mastery in what we do; we can act methodically in response to what faces us, whether it is at home, work or elsewhere; we can stay aware of our progress on the things we are still to complete; and we will know when we have actually completed a task or whether there is more to do.

All of this is relevant to using this book, of course, because gaining the benefits you could from the practices it contains will depend significantly on how goal-directed you are as you use them.

At the same time, it is important to distinguish between what we need to do to achieve a goal (the *action* we need to take) and the goal itself. For example, 'to send a text message', 'to make lunch', 'to attend the meeting', 'to collect the children from school' and 'to set out to go to work' are all examples of the action required to achieve a goal, not of the goal itself.

The goals would be 'sent a text message', 'made lunch', 'attended the meeting', 'collected the children from school' and 'went to work'.

This is an important distinction, which the following 'Defining Goals' figure illustrates. Notice the difference in orientation between the two: between 'aiming at the bull's-eye in order to hit it' (part of what we need to do to achieve the result) and 'the arrow is in the bull's-eye' (the intended outcome of our action, i.e., the actual goal).

Being clear on our goals in these terms promotes success. Failure to do so frequently means that we don't have a complete understanding of what we are setting out to achieve. By contrast, when this distinction is understood we will seek to know the whole intended outcome or end result right from the start (see Chapter 6).

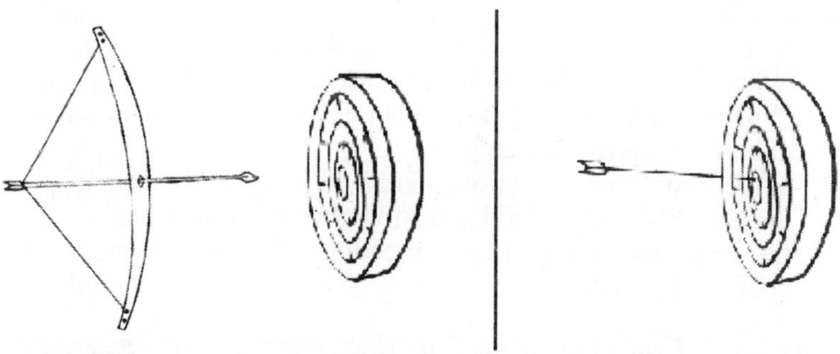

Defining Goals

Exercise 2: Defining Goals. Think of three simple things you need to do today and note them in your logbook as goals. At least one of them could be a direct contribution to your personal wellbeing. Define these goals by describing the end result, not the process of getting that result.

Goals are influenced by many factors; they don't stand alone. Accordingly, various things can interfere with what we do to achieve our goals, such as the scarcity of necessary items, and it is helpful to anticipate these. Also, using available support can make things much easier: experienced people may be willing to help; or others with resources such as money or equipment might readily provide them if they are asked. At the same time, setting out to do something that will predictably fail is a waste of effort: a goal may be impossible or impractical; people with the necessary skills and experience may be unavailable; essential material ingredients or resources may be inaccessible; and disruptive influences from people, organisations or the environment may interfere.

Considering the tasks in which our goals are embedded can help us prepare effectively for these kinds of factors.

TASKS

Definition: A task has four aspects: the *goal* to be achieved, the *action* to be taken to achieve it, the *agent* that is responsible for taking the action, and the *context* in which all this is to occur.[18]

By exploring these components we can plan what is needed to ensure our success. Answering four simple questions is the key to doing this:

1. What is to be achieved (the end result)? (Goal)
2. What needs to be done to achieve it? (Action)
3. Who or what (possibly more than one person) needs to act to achieve the goal? (Agent)
4. What people or things are likely to help or hinder achieving the goal; and, what brings together those involved in the task (e.g., recreation, a work meeting, a funeral, a contract, a crisis…)? (Context)

Principle 2: Exploring the tasks in which our goals are embedded helps to ensure we achieve our goals as reliably as possible.

Think of the following simple example, which we will call 'driving to work with a friend.' The goal is 'both of you have arrived at work safely before 8.30am.' If you are driving, 'you' are the agent; if your friend is driving, 'he or she' is the agent. 'The actual driving itself, how you are to meet before leaving, etc' is the action. The context includes 'who owns the car, any other passengers, the road conditions, the condition of the car, the departure time, the traffic density at that time, and the nature of your relationship (friend, boss-employee, child-parent, etc).'

After giving a little thought to these things, it becomes obvious how helpful it can be to do this kind of review. For example, think of how changes in the context (for example, a blocked road) could lead to changes in what you need to do (find an alternate route), which might influence your success (by making you late). Also, as you make your plans, the skill of the driver (agent) may influence the action and the goal. For example, an inexperienced driver during rush hour might require a different route (change in the action), which could also necessitate an earlier or later arrival time (change of goal).

Exercise 3: Defining Two Tasks.

Step 1: Think of two tasks you intend to complete today or tomorrow. At this stage, select simple ones to make your learning easier and to speed up your ability to understand more complicated tasks later on. Maybe choose something as simple as 'watching a special TV program' or 'answering your emails'.

Step 2: In your logbook, briefly record your answers to the four questions. Keep them simple and notice how they lead to a greater understanding of what is involved and to possible modifications of your plans. These changes are part of the process, so go with them.

Step 3: When you are satisfied that you understand the tasks well enough to proceed, you need to answer a fifth question: What is the first thing I need to do to get started? Using your answer, plan how, when and where you will do that first thing.

Step 4: Commit yourself to doing it and act.

These two simple ideas – goal and task – have helped many disorganised people turn their lives around. Their simplicity is their strength, not their weakness. All the same, balance is important. The fulfilment of the Infinite is realised through *being* not *doing*, and too much emphasis on goal-setting and achievement can block this. Also, if people addicted to work and busyness are to live balanced lives, they need to learn to cultivate spontaneous activity, to flow with Life and not stifle it with over-planning.

6
Guidelines for Goal-Setting

'Everything I start to do just seems to fall into place. When I need money, it's there.'

'I'm never satisfied. I always find fault with what I do.'

'I want my life to be easy, but underneath I don't expect it ever will be.'

'My parents were always ill, so I guess I will be too.'

Human beings are wondrously creative. Our powers are profound. One dimension of this is the way our attitudes largely determine the outcome of everything we undertake in our lives. They influence everything we do and everything we set out to achieve. We can summarise these influences with the following four basic principles.

Principle 1: Where we start is where we finish, unless we change our goals.
This means that our thoughts, feelings, attitudes and expectations at the beginning of any project, task, sequence of events, or set of acts strongly determine the outcome. What we expect at the start, we get at the finish. However, because we are not completely controlled by our initial positions, we can change our goals and achieve different outcomes from those we imagined in the beginning.

Exercise 1: Our Starting and Finishing Positions. You can test this for yourself. Think about your life: Is there anything you have set out to do where this principle did not apply? As you consider this, remember that your attitudes and expectations include those you are aware of and possibly others hidden below the surface of your awareness. Also, remember that there is a difference between wanting something and expecting to have it. Make a record in your logbook.

Principle 2: What we concentrate on is what we get.
This important principle applies to every waking moment. What we keep our attention on becomes more energised the longer we

continue to give it attention (see Chapter 12). This works well for us, when, for example, we choose to concentrate on success, competence, happiness, fulfilment, physical health and wellbeing, because these are then increasingly likely to enter our lives. By contrast, it doesn't work so well when we continue to concentrate on failure, incompetence, unhappiness, yearning, physical discomfort and ill health.

Exercise 2: Self-Fulfilling Attitudes. Think of people you know who seem to have fulfilled this principle. Maybe they talk a lot about, for example, wanting to be successful, healthy, or having a partner in life. But we notice that they are preoccupied with failure, ill health, and being single, and that their lives reflect this. Assess your own goals and preoccupations in the same way by identifying differences between what you would like and what you actually concentrate on. Record your discoveries in your logbook.

Principle 3: We tend to get what we expect in life.
Expectations involve a level of commitment to the outcomes we contemplate, which is not present in vague thoughts. As a result, if we expect to succeed, then generally we do; if we expect to fail, then generally we will do that too; when we expect to complete something by a certain time, or don't expect to get it finished in that time, then generally we fulfil these expectations; also, if we expect our lives to turn out a certain way, then generally that is what happens.

Exercise 3: Self-Fulfilling Expectations. As in Exercise 1, you can check your own life to see if this principle is true. While checking, remember again that sometimes we have mixed reactions, and that all attitudes and expectations, even the hidden ones, contribute to the outcomes we get. On the surface we might 'really want something' or 'really expect that what we want will occur'; however, underlying that may be an expectation of trouble or doubt that we will ever get what we hope for.

Principle 4: We tend to get results in the way (how) we expect to get them.
This principle applies to how we reach our goals or live our lives, and the manner or ease in which we do so. Consider some examples. If we expect (imagine, think, or feel) that something will

be easy or difficult, then generally it turns out the way we expect it will. If we expect something will take a long time, but that we will get there in the end, then generally events unfold like this. If we expect something can only arise when others are involved, then generally we will only get it if others intervene.

Exercise 4: Expectations of How Things Will Occur. Examine your life and remember times when your expectations were fulfilled. Be honest with yourself. Were they actually fulfilled or not? As already mentioned, when we have mixed expectations, feelings, thoughts and impulses, it is the mixture that influences the outcome. Generally, too, if you didn't get the outcome you expected, then you are very likely to have had mixed expectations of some sort. Record what you discover in your logbook.

These four principles can help us to become happier and more fulfilled. We can learn to guide our attention and expectations onto what will work for us. Regrettably, not everyone initially understands their potential for doing this. However, with practice, we can learn to manage our attention by concentrating on other things, and so cultivate expectations that will support what is good for us. This is the inner equivalent of looking from one object to another, listening to different sounds outside us, or touching different textures and noticing the differences.

GUIDELINES FOR GOAL-SETTING

The last four principles have general application. They can also be adapted specifically to help us when we are formulating our goals.[19] Expressed as guidelines, these adaptations can help us to use all of our talents and inner resources when goal-setting.

Guideline 1: Imagine your goals as already completed. We imagine our goals have already occurred or are occurring. There is great power in doing this, because it commits us to the desired outcome as an established fact. We can capture this result by using the present tense: 'I own a new car', 'My family is happy' or 'My job is satisfying'. Using the future or past tense makes the completion less immediate or attainable.

Guideline 2: Concentrate on what you want at completion. This helps us to energise what we want or require, rather than what we don't want or require. A common mistake is to define goals in negative terms and so energise what we don't want: 'not unhappy', 'not arguing', 'not overweight' or 'not being poorly paid'.

We are best to imagine 'being happy', 'cooperating', 'being, say, 60 kilos/132 pounds' or 'being well paid'.

Guideline 3: Imagine that completing the goal was easy. While defining our goals in the present tense, we imagine that in the process of achieving them everything we needed was available exactly when and where it was needed. Everything fell into place. People were available, paperwork was done, contracts were signed, skies were clear, transport arrived punctually, people were happy to help – whatever was necessary or helpful was available easily.

Guideline 4: Use I-Am affirmations to mobilise your life energy. These affirmations enable us to saturate our intentions with fundamental aliveness. They open us to profound influences that support our intent. When we use the words 'I-Am', we energise our worldly interests with vital force or life energy from the Infinite. Remember (from Chapter 4) that I-Am is the aspect of our consciousness that participates in the Infinite as much as possible while we are alive. By adding what we want after 'I-Am', we give shape and direction to the life energy that using 'I-Am' has attracted.

Put another way, affirming I-Am activates our awareness to the empowerment ever present from the Infinite. In our day-to-day lives, this can be like turning on a switch and being flooded with life energy in various guises – intense sensations, feelings, thoughts, memories, understanding, inspirations, transcendence and other phenomena (see Chapters 11 and 12).

Formulating and repeating an I-Am affirmation is, therefore, a powerful way of supporting our success with any goal. For example, worldly goals could include 'I-Am a skilled business person', 'I-Am the successful sale of my car', 'I-Am confident' or 'I-Am a loving parent'; while spiritual goals might include 'I-Am Love', 'I-Am the mastery of this meditation', 'I-Am whole' and 'I-Am Enlightened' (see Chapter 29).

Guideline 5: Do something that you would do if your goal had already been achieved. Doing this helps to materialise or manifest our goals in our lives. It brings the energy of our internal intentions, commitments and affirmations out into the physical world – into our daily lives. Notice this step; it is important. Leaving it out will significantly reduce the likelihood of your success. What you do might seem trivial or insignificant to you. This doesn't matter. The main thing is to do something *physical* that is consistent with success. This needs to involve a physical act: writing a letter, saying something friendly, buying a newspaper, driving a car, making a telephone call, or spending some money. Just imagining such acts is not enough.

Guideline 6: Imagine your success and that you are celebrating it in whatever way is meaningful and enjoyable for you. Make sure that what you imagine is pleasurable and is related to the achievement of your goal. Interestingly, imagining that you are celebrating with others promotes the outcome you want more than imagining you are doing it alone.

Exercise 1: Use the Six Guidelines to Specify a Personal Goal. Think of a simple goal that you would like to achieve, preferably not something you have been trying to do for years or months! Then specify your goal using the six guidelines:

- Imagine your goal is already complete.
- Concentrate on what you want.
- Imagine it was all done easily.
- Compose and use an I-Am affirmation.
- Do something active that aligns with and expresses your success.
- Create a (shared) celebration.

Get yourself grounded at the end (see Chapters 9 and 10). Keep records in your logbook and use them to assess your progress.

A final thought: Once you have decided on a goal, remember that you can change it. We need to be flexible at times because situations change or unexpected outcomes occur that were not part of our original planning. All the same, before you do this, double-check that you are not simply changing the goal because you are reluctant to do what is required to achieve it!

7
KNOWING OUR PRIORITIES

Dr Stephen Covey (author and educator) has recounted a wonderful story for illustrating our life's priorities[20]*:*

An expert in time management is standing in front of an audience of corporate executives. He pulls out a big jar and puts it on a table in front of him. Then he puts as many fist-sized rocks into the jar as he can and asks, 'Is the jar full?' and they all shout, 'Yes!'

Then he produces some gravel and empties that into the jar, shaking it around so he gets as much gravel in as he can. He asks the same question: 'Is the jar full?' Less certainly this time, some say, 'Probably not.'

At this point, he produces some sand and proceeds to put as much sand into the jar as he can, again shaking the jar to do this. 'Is the jar full now?' he asks again. They all say, 'No.'

And then he gets a pitcher and pours water carefully into the jar until it will take no more. At this point he asks: 'What is the point of this illustration?'

Someone answers, 'No matter how busy you are, you can always fit in something more.'

And the expert says something like, 'No. The lesson is: If you don't put the big rocks in first, you'll never get them in. And the big rocks are your important priorities in life: your family, your health, your spiritual nourishment, mentoring and things like that.'

THE BIG ROCKS

This is a wonderfully graphic and eloquent way of describing a common challenge for people in today's world. The challenge is to make sure that we get our priorities right and do what is necessary to fulfil those priorities first. If we don't, we will not be able to make space for them in a life already filled with a mass of other less significant things.

After many years counselling hardworking people, I landed in hospital and discovered that, like them, my health, family life and general wellbeing were suffering because of how busy I was. It was an important wake-up call, which I heard and acted upon. I have also met many people who were hungry or thirsty for the 'soul nourishment' that comes from a regular spiritual practice. But many of them were struggling to keep up their practices because of the day-to-day pressures on them – the presence of the gravel, sand and water in their jars.

Exercise 1: Big Rocks/Ideal Priorities. Give some thought now to what your 'big rocks' – your highest priorities – are. Make a list using summary words like: 'family', 'friends', 'home life', 'intellectual stimulation', 'physical, emotional and mental health', and 'work'. Write whatever seems important to you. When done, order your list from your highest to lowest priority. Then make brief notes of what you currently do about them and how much time you spend on each in an average week or month.

This exercise often surprises people. Many find a mismatch between what they regard as fundamentally important in their lives and the way they live. This mismatch is very significant and we need to find some way of dealing with it if we are to experience ongoing wellbeing. And one way is to discover what our *actual* priorities are and compare them with our *ideal* priorities.

Principle 1: The time we spend on any activity compared with the time we spend on others indicates its actual priority in our lives: The more time spent, the higher the priority.

Exercise 2: Actual Priorities. Assess your average month and estimate the time you spend on your different activities; for example, sleeping, eating, exercise, family, leisure, friends, work or spiritual practice. Order your list so that the ones on which you spend most time are at the top and the ones taking the least time are at the bottom. Compare this list with your *ideal-priority list* from the last exercise. Record what you find in your logbook.

Much of this book is designed to help you to reorganise your priorities when necessary. It does this by providing you with the information and the know-how to assess the current balance of your life. It also offers tried and tested ways of practically meeting your needs. So if your ideal priorities don't match your actual priorities you are likely to find something here that will help you to reorganise your activities so they better support your wellbeing.

Ongoing health and wellbeing depend on regular attention to the full range of our actual needs. Experience shows that we need to: take care of our bodies (eat, sleep and exercise well); obtain enough food, water and shelter (often through working for money these days); take care of our feelings and emotions (find emotional balance and the unique nourishment that comes from feelings); have close emotional contact with others (time with family and close friends); have a sense of presence in who and what we are (to have ways of centring instead of getting lost in external interests and concerns); and experience the fundamental aliveness, fulfilment, healing and completion that come from the Infinite through I-Am, and, for some, eventually to become the Infinite (to have spiritual practices that open us to and enable us to be fully who and what we are).

These activities require daily attention for the whole of our lives. When we don't give them that attention, our aliveness diminishes and we start to suffer in some way. From that point of view, then, these needs should be ranked as our highest priorities. They go at the top of both our *ideal-priority list* and our *actual-priority list*, and we need to spend time in direct proportion to those priorities.

Exercise 3: Changing Priorities. Do at least one thing today to take better care of yourself. Record what you do in your logbook. Also, feel free to do more than one thing! Remember to keep what you do small and manageable. The point of this exercise is for you to ensure that taking better care of yourself is a regular part of each day, and that you make any necessary changes gradually. If you start by doing something too demanding or extreme, for example, you may be less likely to keep up the practice. Make a note of what you will do tomorrow as well.

Long-Term, Medium-Term and Short-Term Goals

When setting our goals, we need to remember to take into account how long they will take to complete. This will help us decide on the order in which to do them:

- *Long-term goals* take years to complete, sometimes a lifetime. They may have a specific end point (e.g., the mortgage is paid off or the training course is finished); or, like the requirements of self-care, they may arise regularly (e.g., doing what is necessary to raise the children, keeping in contact with friends, or meditating).

- *Medium-term goals* take less time, perhaps somewhere between three months and a year. (You decide how long this is for yourself.) They are goals we would expect to complete in that amount of time (e.g., moved house, changed jobs, completed a particular project, or taken a vacation with the family).
- *Short-term goals* are things we would do today, tomorrow, this week, next week, but not much longer than that. (Again, you decide how long this is for yourself.) For example, shopping is done, lunch is eaten, the important phone call made, the day is planned, or you are at work.

There are many advantages to this way of approaching goals. In particular, when planning to complete long- and medium-term goals, it is easy to divide them into a series of shorter-term goals.[21]

Identifying these shorter-term goals helps us to clarify the steps we need to take one at a time as part of achieving our bigger goals. This step-wise approach also helps us to:

- stay systematic and effective.
- make achieving our long- and medium-term goals easier to manage.
- review our progress much more easily and celebrate our successes along the way.
- keep us on track or focused over extended periods..

Having set a medium- or long-term goal, we can make sure we complete a shorter-term goal every day, week, or month that acts as another step towards achieving our bigger goal. In other words, we can set short- or medium-term goals that help us to make progress on our overall goals.

We can also work backwards from our long-term goals to ensure we complete in the medium term and the short term what is required for them. For example, we may have the long-term goal of having regularly spent time with our families, of having succeeded in business, or of having realised spiritual awakening. To achieve each of these goals, we could set a short-term goal every week, such as having spent three evenings and one day of the weekend with the family, having met specified income or project targets for each week, or having engaged in a daily spiritual practice that is part of our religious or spiritual regime.

Alternatively, or at the same time, we may have a medium-term goal, such as, at least once a year having done something special with the family, having earned an end-of-year bonus at work, or having attended a special religious/spiritual event.

Exercise 4: Defining Long-, Medium- and Short-Term Goals. Note down a brief description of one long-term, one medium-term and one short-term goal in your logbook. Then specify at least one thing – make it as simple as you like – that you will do during this week to further the achievement of the long-term goal, and one thing towards the medium-term goal. Commit yourself to do these things and follow through before the end of the week. Make a practice of doing this! You are likely to be surprised at how much you achieve. You don't need to restrict yourself to one goal, of course!

EMPHASISING WHAT IS IMPORTANT

It makes sense to put more energy and time into those things that are important to us than those that are not. In fact, fulfilling our highest priorities is fundamental to our having an ongoing sense of fulfilment, purpose and wellbeing in our lives. Interestingly, this dimension of wellbeing is usually associated with our long-term goals, rather than our medium- or short-term goals, unless the last two are aligned obviously with achieving our long-term ones.

Our priorities can help us to decide when we will do what is needed in our lives, and clarifying our priorities helps us to make these decisions deliberately and consciously. Our life-long priorities, perhaps those involving several decades or more, help us to decide what to emphasise when formulating our medium-term and short-term ones. This can help to ensure that we don't get to the end of our lives and discover we have missed out on what is fundamentally important to us. Many people do! We will discuss priorities again when we get to decision-making (see Chapter 24).

Exercise 5: Aligning Our Long-, Medium- and Short-Term Goals. (You only need to take a few minutes on this exercise.) Think about your reasons for reading this book.

1. Briefly note in your logbook four goals that you wish to achieve by this reading.
2. Then organise them into long-, medium- and short-term goals.
3. When you have done this, ask yourself, 'Are my long-term goals my highest priority?' If they are not, then add other long-term goals that are.

4. After doing this, arrange or rank your long-term priorities by putting numbers beside each: #1 is the highest priority; #2 is the second highest, and so on.
5. Finally, select one of the goals from your original list – preferably but not necessarily your highest priority, and specify one or more simple, easy goals that you will complete as a way to get started on this bigger goal. Complete this smaller goal as soon as you can. Record the outcomes in your logbook.

A final point: There is no need for everything in our lives to be goal-related. We may at times have generalised goals, such as going with the flow, seeing what turns up without planning for it in advance, day dreaming, waiting for events to guide what we do, or simply being. Give yourself these times.

USING TO-DO LISTS

To-do lists can help us to cope with the mass of things we need to complete every day. They enable us to manage our lives instead of our lives managing us. They offer an immediate indication of what we need to do next, how we are progressing and when we have succeeded.

Definition: A To-Do List is a list of the jobs/tasks/goals that we want or have to complete. It includes our long-, medium- and short-term goals.

Without a to-do list we will often only have a vague idea at best of what we still need to do and whether what we have done is actually contributing to our success. At the same time, remember that to-do lists are best used as tools for making our lives easier and richer, not for weighing us down with impossible expectations.

To-do lists provide a map of both what lies ahead and the steps that need to be taken to get there. They also offer encouragement every time we remove items from the list. Some people prefer to put a tick or cross beside completed items so they can see everything that is completed and not just everything awaiting attention. To get you started, do the following exercises.

Exercise 6: Beginning a To-Do List. Make a list in your logbook of all the things you need to do today that are more than you would routinely and easily remember to do without prompting. For example: 'go shopping', 'finish the report', 'contact X and Z before lunch' or 'get a progress report on overdue delivery'.

A couple had a long-held goal of owning their own home, but they rarely remembered it when spending their money. The result: They were still tenants. Then they discovered to-do lists and the need to commit to their high-priority goals. They made a joint commitment 'to have bought their own home' (this was their long-term priority goal) and 'to have saved 10% of every pay and put it in a home savings account' (this was their repeating short-term goal). They enjoyed watching the money accumulate and bought their own home within three years!

Exercise 7: Long-, Medium- and Short-Term To-Do Lists. Think of one of your long-term objectives. If you don't have any, invent one. Note it in your logbook. Remember it needs to take more than a year to complete; for example, 'the car loan is paid off ahead of time'. Then write down a medium-term goal you need to complete before the long-term one can be completed; for example, 'to have a part-time job within two months to pay the extra money that is needed'. Finally, think of what you also need to do today or in the next week to find the extra job in order to pay off the car loan; for example, 'went home twice this week to eat instead of eating at an expensive restaurant', 'put the money saved in the bank' or 'looked on the Internet for a part-time job' and 'made at least two telephone calls or sent two emails about jobs before the end of the week'.

Exercise 8: Practising Using To-Do Lists. Create a simple to-do list for this week. Follow the pattern outlined above as you include one long-, one medium- and one short-term goal. Without overloading yourself, also include some other goals that you need to complete each day. Then, having made the list, make a clear decision: 'I will complete these short-term goals today.' Make notes in your logbook about your success.

Doing a *weekly review* of your to-do list is worthwhile. During this, consider your long- and medium-term goals to make sure you are doing what is required to complete them. Also, it helps to do a quick *daily review* of your list, so you can remove completed goals and add others now waiting to be completed. Keep adjusting the priorities of your short-term goals to support greater efficiency, not to avoid doing them!

8
Beginning to Meditate

Millions of meditations are taught in the world. We can get an idea of how big and varied the field is by thinking of cooking because there are at least as many different types of meditation as there are types of cooking. With meditations, for example, there are Buddhist, Christian, Hindu, Kabbalistic, Islamic, Sufic, Shamanic, Shinto, Taoist, Zen, and many other kinds. Within each there are also different schools or streams, and usually within each school (as in cooking) there is a multitude of specific meditations (recipes). A complete encyclopaedia of meditation would be huge.

Many people interested in meditation find such diversity hard to deal with and often have similar questions: *How do I know what meditation I need? Do I need to enrol in a school to learn to meditate? Isn't there just one simple meditation that I can use? I'd love to do it, but how can I stop being put off by how complicated it all seems?*

The answer to all of these questions is the same: Take all the time you need to find out.

Like any area of substance in life, when we first discover it we may feel intimidated by how much there is to learn and how long it will take us. However, this reaction involves expecting ourselves to start at the end of our learning when we will know a lot, not at the beginning when we know very little. At the beginning, we do the ABCs, then we progress to single words, and then to phrases, and then to sentences. Eventually, we may write a brilliant literary work, but not in the beginning.

Accordingly, this beginning chapter contains meditational ABCs. Encouragingly, there are only three essential elements to all or most meditations.

EVERYDAY MEDITATIONS

Surprisingly, when we learn what meditation is, many of us discover that we are already meditating in a variety of ways every day, although we may not call it that. Here are a few examples:

- You are cooking a meal, playing sport, or doing something at work, and you notice what you are doing and that you are tired.

- You are lying or sitting somewhere comfortable, in the sun maybe, and notice that you are allowing your thoughts and feelings to drift.
- You are involved in something you enjoy intensely and keep noticing what you enjoy and that you are enjoying it.
- You are thinking about a problem, wondering how you will solve it, and regularly notice that you are doing well or not so well.

THREE KEY INGREDIENTS

Each of these examples involves meditation, because each of them has three key ingredients: *sustained attention*, a *subject/object/process* and *self-awareness*.

Definition: We are meditating when we pay sustained self-aware attention to a subject, object or process.

Put another way, many everyday activities are meditations because during them we remain attentive (sustained attention) to something (a subject, object or process) and are aware that we are doing so at the time (self-awareness). Just take a moment to think of the number of times a day you do this. As you think about it, also let yourself realise that, although your attention may lapse from time to time, ongoing attention is present in much of what you do.

Meditation 1: Three Ingredients. Experiment with this now. As you sit with this book in your hands or on your screen, keep looking at or feeling (sustained attention) the book (subject/ object/ process), and be aware that you are doing this (self-awareness). Describe what this is like in your logbook. To practise more, you can do this with anything else you can see, hear or touch right now.

Sustained Attention

Sustaining our awareness is central to many parts of life and we learn to do it from a very young age. For example, we learn to pay attention when we do school work, solve a problem at work, compile a shopping list, decide which TV programs to watch, wonder about our jobs, plan a vacation, or when thinking about something that we would like to change. Of course, some people are better at this than others. However, you would not be reading this book unless you were capable of doing it, at least a little.

During meditation, what we do is both very similar to these kinds of activities and a bit different. In everyday life we often give ourselves freedom to think of other things, to accept interruptions, or to allow our attention to wander. When meditating, by contrast, we intend to concentrate on the subject/object/process of the meditation for as long as we are meditating. Even if we are interrupted, we deliberately keep bringing our attention back to whatever it is. And with practice this gets easier.

As a result, during meditation, our attention is actively engaged in the process; it is not passive. This is like the difference between, for example, deciding to look at some specific aspect of a view, and absorbing it generally without any intent; or between deliberately listening to specific conversations in a crowded room, and passively noticing the overall sound; or between intentionally heading for a particular location, and aimlessly meandering around an area. In everyday terms, paying attention like this, even if just for a few moments at a time in the beginning, can help us to improve our alertness, awareness and concentration.

Meditation 2: Sustained Attention. Sit or stand comfortably and close your eyes. For half a minute or a little more if you want to, think about something that you would like to do today or tomorrow. Make it something as simple and easy as having a cup of coffee, going for a walk or talking to someone. Then encourage yourself to stay relaxed and to stay aware of your subject. Keep internally looking at its different aspects; listening for its various themes, melodies and stories; feeling its impact on you; discussing it with yourself; or allowing the fragrance or essence of it into your awareness. You may be surprised at how rich and varied the experience is. Keep yourself relaxed and, whatever else you may become aware of, keep returning to the subject you have chosen. Make notes in your logbook at the end.

The Subject/Object/Process

When meditating we cultivate awareness of a subject, object or process. These 'items' usually give meaning and direction to our meditations. Importantly, too, while meditating these items can become the central reference or core of everything else we see; the themes around which all else is played; and the points from which we measure everything that we observe. Paying attention to them is often also the way that we gain direct access to the rewards offered to us by particular meditations.

The centre or focus of our meditations can be anything from a shoe to God. To give only a few examples, we might meditate on *a subject* like justice, creation, grace, inner peace, love, or life; on *an object* like a flame, a tree, a person, the sun, money, a car, or a house; or on *a process* like breathing, walking, writing, thinking, making decisions, going with the flow, or repeating a mantra.

Meditation 3: Noticing 'Items' in Your Awareness.

Step 1: Sit or stand comfortably for a few minutes and allow your attention to range over whatever you are experiencing. As you do, notice the variety that comes into your awareness. For example, you might notice physical sensations, inner pictures, people and events around you, memories from earlier in the day, feelings or thoughts, impulses or desires, fantasies about the future. Whatever is in the field of your awareness, notice it.

Step 2: Each time you notice something, accept its presence and let it be. Avoid doing anything active with it like thinking about it or analysing it. Imagine it is like a movie or play that you are witnessing and notice how it unfolds and changes without your doing anything. Then when it goes from your awareness, let it go easily. Other things will arise. Observe the variety and richness in your awareness. Make notes in your logbook.

Self-Aware Attention

When meditating, we cultivate self-aware attention; we practise noticing what we are doing as we do it. Put another way, we practise remaining aware both of *what we are doing* and *that we are doing it*. Self-aware attention only arises when we do both. In everyday terms, this kind of attention helps us to become centred, alert and more perceptive in our lives.

Meditation is not just daydreaming. In daydreaming we allow our attention to do whatever it wants without guiding it or expecting to remain aware of what we are doing. We are *lost* in the dream, instead of being *alert* in the dream. For many people, the whole of life is a daydream. Of course, there is value in 'alert daydreaming', which can be wonderfully restoring and insightful.

We also tend to lose self-awareness when we become so absorbed in an activity that it takes over and we no longer know we are engaged in it. Test yourself with the following. You have just read these words. As you did, were you aware that you were reading them? Or were you just reading? To explore further, think back and remember what you were thinking or feeling as you read other parts of this book. Did you read and notice what was happening in and around you at the time or not?

The good news is that most people find this self-awareness very easy, even with only short practice periods, and many of us do it spontaneously. Examples might include when we are learning new things and have to stay aware of how we are approaching them, or when we are self-conscious or nervous about what we are doing.

Meditation 4: Self-Aware Attention.

Step 1: Become aware at this moment of exactly what you are doing. How long have you been doing it? Also notice where you are. Are you sitting or standing? What is going on around you?

Step 2: Keep noticing where you are and what is going on around you. And as you do, notice that you are noticing. This will give you both awareness of what you are noticing and awareness that you are noticing it, the two essential ingredients in self-aware attention. Practice this. Make notes in your logbook.

EASY MEDITATION

Meditation 5: Full Meditation. Begin by noticing where you are and what is around you; also, notice the sensations in your body and pay deliberate attention to these. You only need to do this for a short time. While you do it, select something in your field of awareness: something in the world around you, or some experience you are having internally. Keep paying attention to whatever this is and, as you do, notice that you are doing all of this. You may be pleasantly surprised at how calming and invigorating this simple meditation is. Record what you notice in your logbook when you finish.

9
Grounding: A Life-Changing Meditation

In this chapter, we explore a meditation that has changed the lives of many thousands of people who used it regularly. Called *grounding*[22], even using it irregularly can make life easier and more fulfilling in undreamt of ways. This may seem like an extreme claim, but I don't make it lightly.

A challenge: Do the *grounding meditation* regularly for the next six months during your waking hours. You only need to do it for three to five seconds at a time. Of course, you can do it for longer if you wish. By the end, you can discover for yourself how amazingly more balanced, easier and more rewarding your life is. Many people have. The more frequently you do it (say, every 15, 30 or 60 minutes), the greater the rewards.

Grounding is a simple, natural process involving physical awareness. Grounding ourselves is a wonderful way to live in the here-and-now: the emphasis on the physical world surrounding us is *here*, while all current attention to the physical is *now*. It also helps us to maintain physical, emotional and mental equilibrium. When well grounded, we generally experience ease, harmony, light and fragrance more intensely and more often. At the same time, discomfort, disharmony, dullness and unpleasantness tend to be digested and disappear. These outcomes clearly make grounding a wonderful way to improve our wellbeing.

> *'Grounding has changed my life. As you predicted, I could never have guessed what a difference it was going to make to me when I started. It's wonderful!'*

> *'Grounding is the most powerful way of coping with life, keeping myself balanced and handling challenges that I have ever learnt.'*

> *'Even after many years of meditating and learning very advanced practices, grounding remains my central meditation, the one I do with everything.'*

WHAT GROUNDING IS

Grounding connects us to our bodies and the physical world. When grounded we always have some physical awareness of what is happening inside and around us, and any exchanges between the two. This awareness does not need to dominate the rest of our attention. It is enough for it to be there, accompanying everything else that we are noticing. So, for example, we can be making plans, enjoying ourselves, talking to others, driving a car – doing anything – whilst staying aware physically.

A naturally occurring process, grounding becomes a meditation as we sustain our attention on the physical aspects of our experience and stay aware that we are doing this as we do it.

Definition: We are grounded when we are aware of the physical sensations in our bodies, the physical things and events around us, and the physical exchanges between the two.

Meditation 1: Grounding – Inside First, then Outside.

Step 1: Do it now. Become aware of the contact of your body with what is supporting you: the pressure in your buttocks or your back, and the sensations in your feet on the floor. You may be aware of other sensations as well, for example, in your stomach, near your diaphragm, or in your arms or legs, neck or head. Notice whatever is there at the same time as noticing your body contact with what is supporting you. Keep doing this for a short time.

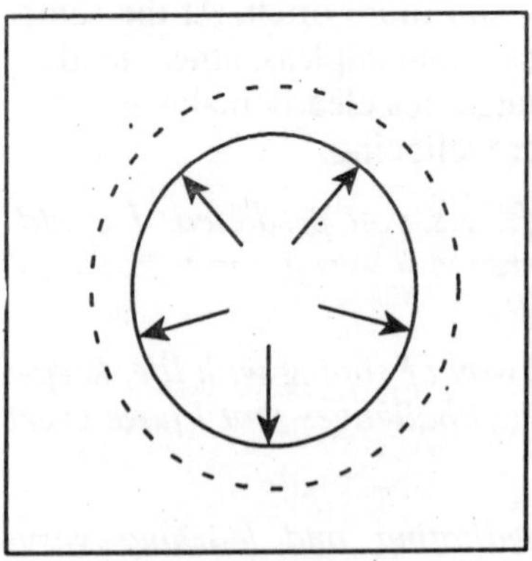

Awareness of 'Inner' Physical Experience

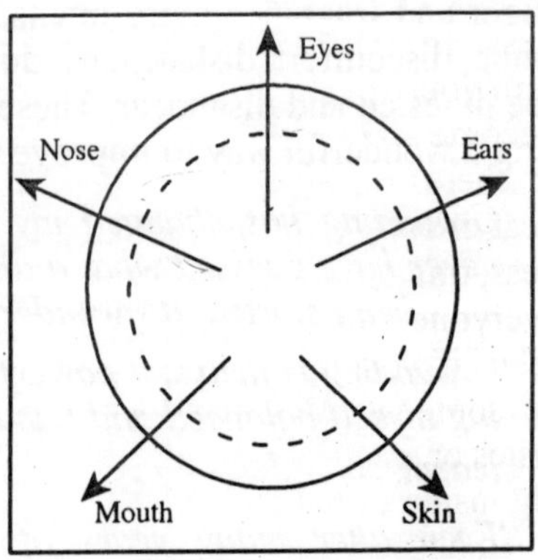

Awareness of 'Outer' Physical Experience

Step 2: Start to look around you and see what is there, listen to any sounds you can hear, notice any fragrances you can smell, any tastes in your mouth, and reach out and touch things.

Step 3: See, hear, feel or talk about the physical connections or exchanges between the inside and outside. Create them if they don't seem to be there.

Step 4: Use your logbook to record any change in your experience. Maybe you are feeling calmer, quieter and easier; maybe the world around you looks brighter, sounds softer, and feels fresher, maybe not.

Relax if you discover the experiences inside your body are very subtle or seem non-existent at times. This is perfectly normal and still sufficient to experience the benefits of grounding. Even 'the nothing' you are aware of inside you is a sensation.

HOW TO GROUND YOURSELF

As already mentioned, grounding is a natural process and being grounded is a natural state, so the first thing to understand is that there is very little for you to do. Also, you don't need to learn to do this, nor to concentrate hard as you do. So when grounding yourself, if you find that you are putting effort into it then you are probably trying too hard. Your body will do it all for you, if you will simply let it do what it is designed to do. All the same, you may need to learn is how to let it do it. This is discussed later.

The way to do the grounding is to notice anything that is physically occurring inside you, what is physically outside you, and to link the two in your awareness. To notice the inside, you turn your attention inwards and become aware of the sensations in there. For example, notice heat or cold, tightness or looseness, tingling or numbness. Not everyone feels sensations, so relax if you don't. You might be someone who sees, hears, tastes or smells what is happening inside you.

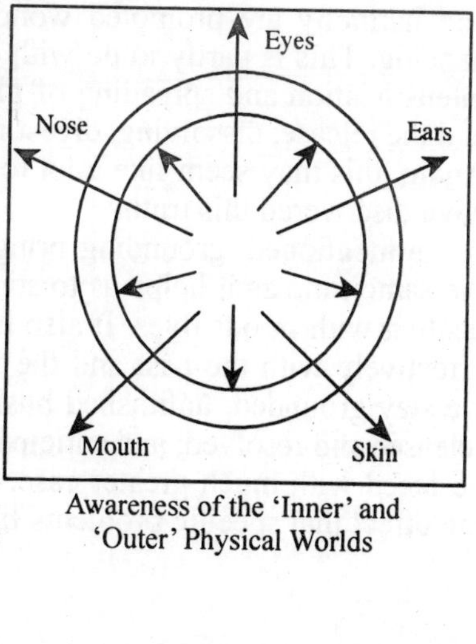

Awareness of the 'Inner' and 'Outer' Physical Worlds

To notice the outside, you use your five sense organs – eyes, ears, skin, nose and mouth – to observe the people, things and events around you. You guide your attention onto colours, shapes, positions, sounds, textures, heat and cold, fragrances and tastes. You look at, listen to, touch, taste and smell what is around you.

It is worth remembering that our inner and outer awareness is always there, as are discernible exchanges between the two. Also, when we turn our attention to it, this awareness intensifies and we gain great benefits from that intensification.

Meditation 2: Grounding – Outside First and then Inside. This time, start with noticing what is going on around you. Be aware that what you see, hear, feel, taste and smell is immediate and automatic. There is no waiting. The moment you give your attention to something, it is there. (If you have sensory problems this may not be as easy as I have just described.) Now, while you continue noticing the outside physical world, also pay attention to what is physically occurring inside your body. Do this as you did in *Meditation 1*. Then pay attention to the physical connections or exchanges between the two: perhaps a natural flow between the two, or a stable, seamless oneness, or even a disconnection that you notice, which is paradoxically also a connection. After a few minutes, less if you are pressed for time, stop and record any changes you observe in your sense of wellbeing in your logbook.

BENEFITS

Grounding has many benefits. The best overall results are that our general life balance, wellbeing, contentment, happiness, clarity and harmony are promoted wonderfully. Grounding is life enhancing. This is partly to do with the way it encourages both the intensification and spreading of pleasure, comfort and aliveness, and the release, dissolving, digesting and removing of discomfort. Again, this may seem like a lot to claim. However, many people have discovered this truth.

As mentioned, grounding brings us into the here-and-now at the same time as it helps us to stay concentrated on what we are dealing with in our lives. It also helps us to deal powerfully and effectively with the past and the future (see Chapter 10). When we stay grounded, unfinished business from the past is digested, released and resolved; and anticipated difficulties in the future can be faced with much greater ease. It has such a powerful balancing effect that specific problems like anxiety or panic attacks will often resolve in seconds or minutes.

When grounded, our automatic processes also take care of our feelings and thoughts in a natural way.[23] Emotional balance is established or restored, clear thinking is promoted, and confusion and other difficulties with thinking clear up. Encouraging ourselves to stay grounded also supports relaxed healthy living, promotes aliveness and vitality, helps us to deal calmly and effectively with difficult people or situations, releases stress, helps us to solve all sorts of personal problems, and promotes our staying steady even when challenged strongly. Through grounding we connect to 'who we are' by our direct inner experiences balancing with our connection to the outside world through our senses. All our energies – bodily, feeling, thinking and spiritual – are digested and integrated.

10
Living With Grounding

The benefits of grounding are yours as soon as you start to do it, and the more often you do it, the more they can become an ongoing part of your life (see Chapter 9). At the same time, stay relaxed as you start your learning; there is no need to pressure yourself into anything. Each time you get grounded, you will add to the benefits you have already had from doing it.

Also, as you practise grounding, remember that you are not learning anything new. Our bodies and the rest of our systems already know how to stay grounded; in fact, our systems crave grounding all the time. So, what you will be learning is how to allow your system to do what it does naturally when left to itself, which may involve unlearning habits that interfere with the process.

There is a recording called the *Grounding Meditation* that is a wonderful aid in learning.[24] Grounding itself, however, does not require a recording, so we encourage you to practise grounding at every opportunity, starting today. You can do this in a matter of seconds. Do it now: take a few moments to become aware of the physical sensations in your body, of what is going on around you, and of their physical connectedness to each other. It only takes a few seconds; and that is basically all there is to it.

REMINDING YOURSELF TO GET GROUNDED

The best results come as we increasingly embed grounding into our lives. This helps us to make it an automatic accompaniment to all that we do. We can do this by reminding ourselves to get grounded regularly, no matter what is going on at the time. The following recommendations might help you to get started.

Reminder 1: Choose one or more incidents that are regularly repeated during your day. Every time they occur, take a few seconds to concentrate on grounding: the telephone rings, you are stopped at traffic lights, the baby cries or the children are upset, you sip a drink of coffee/tea/water, etc. Remember that you only need to do the grounding for a few seconds at a time to benefit.

Reminder 2: Set a timer for a particular interval (every 15, 30, or 60 minutes). Every time it goes off, reset it and, as you do, take a few seconds to ground yourself. It is surprising how few people notice the small interruption of the timer, and even if they do, the process of grounding itself is completely private.

Reminder 3: Do it whenever you or others start to feel something intensely. When dealing with strong feelings or disruptive behaviour, yours or others, ground yourself. This is important. There is no need to struggle on bravely when feeling intensely upset or out of sorts.

TEN HELPFUL HINTS TO MAKE IT EASIER

As we gain experience with grounding we discover simple things that help us with the process. By making a list in your logbook, you will have a ready reminder when you need it. The following list is included to help you get started.

Hint 1: Remember to use as many of your senses as possible. For example, if touching is not working well, then look or listen for a while; if looking is not working well, listen intently, have a good sniff or reach out and touch something.

Hint 2: Movement is usually helpful. If you cannot actually move around from place to place, then shift your position so your sensations are more noticeable and your energy releases more rapidly. Swimming, running, walking, digging in the garden, household jobs and other similar activities are all helpful from time to time, too, especially if we have strong feelings.

Hint 3: If you find sensations persist or seem to linger in your body, move the parts of your body involved and the parts of your body next to them, to encourage the sensations to release (arms, legs, neck, head, torso etc). This works well to bring relief.

Hint 4: Consider doing something specific and stimulating if you are in special need of strong grounding. For example, reach out and hold something very strongly; suck a lemon; sip a tart drink; have alternating hot and cold showers; listen to loud, stimulating music; look at bright or flashing lights, or go out into the sunlight. The idea is to match the intensity of your experience with the intensity of your connection to the world around you, and to experience exchanges between the two.

Hint 5: As a quick grounding technique, notice your feet on the floor or ground, or your buttocks on your seat.

Hint 6: Pay attention to a particular part of your body. The longer you do, the more sensation you will detect there.

Hint 7: Notice any sensations that immediately attract your attention, even if they are only mild or it is 'the sensation of nothing.' Notice where it is and how it changes.

Hint 8: We do not all feel sensations or the connections between the inside and outside. So yours may be more obvious by looking for them inside you, or by listening for the sounds they make, or by tasting or smelling them. Alternatively, they may be more obvious when you talk about them to yourself.

Hint 9: Grounding is to do with the physical aspects of your experience, so if you find anything troublesome is persisting – thoughts, feelings, sensations, memories, impulses, or desires – to digest and release them, immediately pay attention to your bodily sensations, to the physical world around you and to their linkages.

Hint 10: If you are feeling something very intensely then concentrate your primary attention on the outside; if you are over-attentive to the outside, concentrate your primary attention on the inside. This hint helps us when our attention is unbalanced. Remember, grounding works best when we are simultaneously aware of the inside and outside, and the exchanges between them.

MANAGING PAST, FUTURE OR PRESENT CHALLENGES

We have already mentioned that grounding is an effective way of releasing unfinished business from the past and for helping us to prepare for the future with equanimity and optimism. There are several simple meditations that you can practise to help you do these things. Using the *Grounding Meditation* recording is again often particularly helpful when we are stressed, because following the spoken instructions releases us from needing to keep remembering what to do next.

Dealing with the Past

Meditation 1: Digesting Past Experiences.

Step 1: Remember an uncomfortable event in your recent past that is still unresolved, and relive it as fully as you can.

Step 2: After a short time, set aside your memory and get yourself grounded. Remind yourself that grounding involves concentrating primarily on your physical sensations, the physical world around you, and the bodily linkages between the two.

Step 3: When you are calmer, relive the event again. Notice any differences in your experience, then again get yourself grounded.

Step 4: Keep repeating this sequence until you no longer remember the incident, you are at ease with the memory, or your feelings about it are neutral. If your responses were very intense or long-standing, you may need to repeat the above steps regularly as the days pass. Each repetition will make a difference, even when you don't notice it. Make notes in your logbook.

Dealing with the Future

Meditation 2: Digesting Fantasies about the Future.

Step 1: Think about the future. Identify something you are going to do about which you feel uncomfortable, or someone you need to meet who will be a challenge for you. Notice what you anticipate is going to happen.

Step 2: After doing this briefly, ground yourself by setting aside your fantasy and relating to your physical sensations. Your sensations will have been stimulated by your imagination. Also, notice the physical world around you, and the connection between the two. Remember to concentrate particularly on the physical, not on your thoughts, feelings and other reactions.

Step 3: After a short time, return to your thoughts or fantasies about the future. Do so briefly, then again get yourself grounded. Continue grounding until you are clearer and more settled. Also notice any differences compared with when you started.

Step 4: Keep repeating this sequence until you can think of the future challenge with confidence or neutrality. If you need to, keep repeating the meditation as the days pass. Gradual progress may be needed rather than a quick fix. Note what you experience in your logbook.

Dealing with Here-and-Now Discomfort

When uncomfortable, we can use current pleasure or memories of past pleasure to enhance the changes grounding promotes. Concentrating on past or present pleasure soothes and heals.

Meditation 3: Dealing with Present Discomfort.

Step 1: If you notice you are uncomfortable about something, the first step is to get yourself grounded. Then, as you keep doing this, think back and remember an experience that was very pleasant for you. Alternatively, notice anything right at the time that is pleasing to you.

Step 2: To intensify the pleasure you feel, remember any fragrances or smells that accompanied the past experience, or what you can smell in the here-and-now. Keep yourself grounded as you do this.

Step 3: Continue noticing past or present ease until you start to experience pleasure, light, harmony, sweetness or fragrance. And particularly notice the way in which your pleasure spreads through or intensifies in your system. Practice helps with this meditation, as with the others. Keep notes in your logbook so you can track your progress.

11
Centring: Harnessing Our Personal Power

Centred people attract our attention by radiating poise, presence and vitality. Being well centred in Life, they have a sense of who they are and that they have abundant life energy available to them. This enables them to live in their full power with ease and flow. By contrast, people who are not centred in Life often appear lost, lethargic, weakened – even empty in some way – and often have little or no sense of who they are.

UNDERSTANDING CENTREDNESS

'I'm always preoccupied with what others are thinking about me and try to please everyone, to do the right thing.'

'I'm a very physical person, my body is central to who I am, which is why I spend so much time looking after it.'

'I'm a passionate person. I can't imagine myself without feelings.'

'I'm always in my head. Ask me about feelings and I don't know what you mean. I'm a thinker.'

'When I pay attention to what I am, it's as if nothing is there, and the nothing includes everything that other people talk about to me.'

'I feel I'm one with everything. I don't really understand what others mean about their bodies and physical objects.'

Whether centred in Life or not, people can have a *sense of self* that arises from consistent experiences, experiences that have repeated, usually many times. These may be to do with the attitudes and expectations of others, bodily sensations and capacities, feelings or emotions, ways of thinking about ourselves, awareness of subtle energy, transcendence beyond space and time, or combinations of these. Whatever these experiences were, they have become familiar to us through their repetition, and, once repeated often enough, we identified with them and claimed them as our own. As a result, they became our sense of what or who we are – our sense of self. Once established, this self acts as the foundation that we use as the primary reference in our lives – unless or until it changes, as it can. It is our vehicle for experiencing and understanding ourselves and the world.

In fact there is a great diversity of possible experiences and knowing that are involved in centring. They include that people can be centred in:

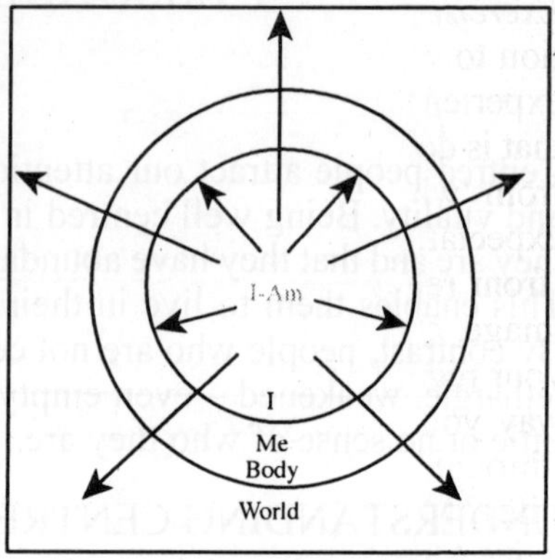

General Types of Centring Experience

- The *world and others* with a self that has arisen through the repeating views expressed about them by others that they take on as their own. For example: 'You are wonderful, talented, fantastic…'; 'You are not okay, hopeless, unintelligent…'; 'You are a thinker, practical...'; 'You are too emotional; too unemotional…'; 'You will succeed in everything you do, always make a mess of things, never amount to anything…'.
- In the *body* through repeating physical sensations, perceptions and practices. For example: flexibility, strength, resilience, stiffness, weakness; attractiveness, ugliness, overweight, skinniness; beautifully proportioned, nose too big, big/small buttocks, eyes too wide/narrow….
- In *me* through repeating feelings, passions and emotions. For example: happiness, equanimity, ease; anger, sullenness, fear, depression; preoccupied with likes and dislikes; optimistic, open, closed; confident, insecure….
- In *I* through repeating thinking and personality patterns. For example: how we perceive ourselves (as good/bad, systematic/chaotic, concerned or disdainful with others, spiritual, practical, socially aware, self-absorbed, generous/selfish, intelligent/silly…).
- In *I-Am* through ongoing experiences of the qualities or states available in the Infinite. For example: timelessness, merging of consciousness, a sense of aliveness of everything, people and objects all one, meaning in everything, space and time (variable and flexible).

To add greater variety, people also often centre in more than one of these dimensions simultaneously or they may move sequentially between them.[25]

Exercise 1: Simple Centring. Take a few moments to pay attention to what you are experiencing right now. As you notice your experience, do you have a sense of self, of who or what you are that is doing the noticing? If you do, does your sense of self derive from 'what others have programmed into you' (their attitudes and expectations, your value in their eyes etc), or arise in your 'body' (from regular physical sensations, physical activities, your body image, etc), in your 'me-ness' (from your feelings about yourself, your regular passions or emotions, etc), in your 'I-ness' (from the way you think, your personality, who you are etc) or as 'I-Am' (through direct knowing of transcendence and the beyond, of Life)? Maybe your sense of self is different from these; if so, what is it? Also, ask yourself, 'Is it stable, or does it keep changing?' Make notes in your logbook.

LIFE ENERGY FROM THE INFINITE

Life energy is always flowing in and through our worldly lives. Our very aliveness, which enables us to do all that we do, is this flow. It maintains, heals and animates us – contributing to and enhancing our wellbeing. It keeps us healthy, balanced, released from the past, free in the future, and eventually, if we make ourselves available to it, it prompts our direct experience and knowing of Life itself – the Infinite.

When combined with grounding, centring keeps us in the I-Am-here-and-now, which gives us full presence in our worldly lives. By combining centring with grounding, we enhance this state through the increased flow of life energy that results in a building abundance of vital force.[26] Significantly, too, it is by continuing to experience whatever is in our awareness that we become better centred in what is familiar to us and, perhaps, beyond that, in I-Am.

In everyday terms, this vital force is familiar. We observe it in the forces of nature and the natural environment. It is also in our physical vitality, our feeling and emotional intensity, our cognitive and personal power, and in our direct presence with I-Am.

To understand the combined effects of centring and grounding, think of an analogy. By concentrating on centring ourselves, we plug our systems into the source of our aliveness, the Infinite, just as we plug an electrical appliance into a live wall socket. By concentrating on grounding, we use our physical awareness of our bodies, of the outside world and of their connectedness, to ensure that we are well earthed in the world, just as all electrical equipment needs to be earthed in order to function fully.

Both connections are necessary. With centring connecting us to the Infinite and grounding to the earth, life energy flows into I-Am and then into the rest of our energetic and bodily systems, clearing the way for and activating our unrealised capacities as it does. It then flows out of our bodies into the world around us. The stronger this flow is, the better our equipment will work, the more saturated with Life we become.

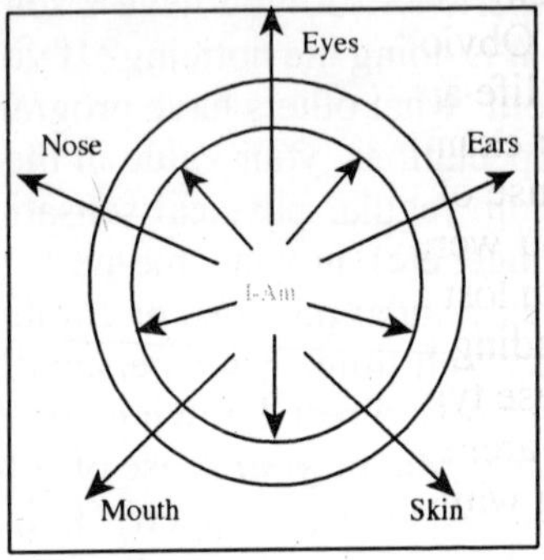

Life Energy Flowing from I-Am in the Infinite through Five Senses into the World

In the diagram, I-Am shows where the primary link with life energy is, the five senses show how we are earthed, and the arrows show energy flow and inner and outer connections.

In addition to the wonderful everyday results of using centring and grounding together, the overall, eventual outcome of combining the two is a developing sense of the fundamental wholeness of everything and an evolving openness to becoming I-Am, our ultimate sense of self. (Chapters 9 to 12 give specific information on the benefits of combining grounding and centring. See also *Meditation 1* in Chapter 19 for how to expand your sense of self.)

TWO WAYS OF CENTRING

To know the wonders of centring, we need to know how to do it. Distinguishing two approaches – *centring-on* and *centring* – helps us to do this.

Centring-On

Centring-on something is very familiar to most people. We are centred-on whatever we are paying primary attention to. For example, as you read this, you are centred-on what you are reading;

if you stop and think for a while about what you have read, you are centred-on what you are thinking; if you look out of the window and focus on a tree or some other object, you are centred-on the tree or object. Importantly, during grounding, it is when we pay attention to our physical sensations, the physical things and events around us, and their sensate linkages – when we are centred-on them – that we get the many benefits of the process.

Obviously, too, we need to pay attention to many other things in life and not doing so can create enormous difficulties. We can, for example, become so centred-on something that we lose a clear sense of what else is occurring in or around us. Remember when you were so absorbed in a novel, movie or computer game that you lost track of where you were and started to live what you were reading or watching as if you were in it. While entertaining with these types of activities, this kind of reaction can lead to a lack of awareness of things to which we need to pay attention. Daydreaming while driving, for example, can be dangerous!

Meditation 1: Centring-On the Outside. Sit or stand comfortably. Keep your eyes open and pay attention to something near you that you can see, hear, touch, taste or smell. Increasingly allow and encourage your attention to become riveted on, consumed by or strongly involved with whatever it is. After doing this for several minutes, notice what, if anything, has happened to your sense of self, and notice anything else you have become unaware of. Record your observations in your logbook.

Centring

Centring itself involves *self-aware attention*, the last of the three basic elements in meditation that we discussed in Chapter 8. We centre by encouraging ourselves to do two things: to remain 'aware that we are aware' and to align with the aspect of us – called the *witness* or *observer* by some people – that is aware. When we refer from now on to our sense of self as our 'witness' or 'observer', its capacities for awareness will be significant.

To experience the fullest possible flooding of life force, we need to align ourselves with this observer at all times, an alignment that comes from paying attention to it as we open our awareness to it. Reducing our awareness of or alignment with our observer reduces the flow of life energy, somewhat like the effect of turning down a dimmer switch on a light (see Chapter 12).

All the same, remember that the spectrum of our life force is very broad and our direct experience of it at a particular time may not reveal all its power to us. Nevertheless, the way the power of Life is available to us is wonderfully simple. All we need to do is to live our awareness of what we are experiencing at any moment. In detail, this means cultivating awareness of whatever we currently experience and know, staying grounded as we do, and *centring* in the *observer* through *self-aware attention*. Whatever these experiences are (including attitudes, physical sensations, feelings, thoughts or something else) they are our direct connection at the time to the source of our aliveness – to I-Am and the Infinite.

Meditation 2: Noticing Your Centre. Sit in a comfortable position and centre-on what is in your awareness. Notice what you are experiencing inside or outside your body, no matter what this is. While continuing to do this, notice any sense you have of what your observer is like? Remember that your observer is the aspect of you that 'is aware that you are aware' – your sense of self. Record your observations in your logbook.

Experientially, the physical or sensate dimension of sense of self may be:

- Specific and stationary.
- In more than one place.
- Moving around inside or outside your body.
- A vertical centre-line behind, in the middle, or in front of your body.
- Defined, obvious, limited.
- A pinpoint.
- Bubbles of openness, quietness, stillness or clarity.
- Excluding or including other aspects of experience.
- Diffuse, subtle or vast.
- Areas of mild to extreme pleasure inside or outside the body.
- Areas of mild to extreme pain or discomfort.
- Vast fields of pure awareness that are part of your fundamental existence in everything.

Some, but by no means all, the possibilities are listed here.

The following meditation combines centring and grounding so you can centre yourself quickly when you need to, just as you now can with grounding. It is an expanded version of *Meditation 2.*

Meditation 3: Centring In Your Sense of Self or Observer.

Step 1: Sit or stand in a comfortable position and get yourself well grounded by becoming aware of your physical sensations, the people, things and events in the world around you and the sensate connections or exchanges between the two of them. This brings you into the here-and-now. Do this for a few minutes, allowing your experiences to unfold in whatever way they do.

Step 2: Then, as you keep grounding yourself, cultivate your 'awareness that you are aware' of your sensations and the world around you. Notice this awareness and any sense of self in you that is aware.

Step 3: No matter what form or non-form this seems to take, encourage yourself to align, become one with or dissolve into it. Doing this brings you into the I-Am-here-and-now. Make notes in your logbook at the end.

12
LIVING WITH CENTRING

Centring is a crucial ingredient in all meditations and, as discussed in the last chapter, it contributes greatly to our lives. It is central to the ongoing self-aware attention that enables our lives to be transformed as we cultivate it. This self-aware attention also enables us to explore and deeply experience aspects of ourselves and anything else of interest to us. It opens up new and wonderful ways of learning that can enrich our lives greatly. For example, when we meditatively become one with what we are learning, we learn through the direct experience of it. We get to know it from the 'inside' by becoming it, which is a very different kind of learning – and more awakened – than 'learning about' a subject.

> *Many years ago, Swami Krishna Gautam, one of my meditation masters, explained this to a group of us during a teaching session. Referring to an analogy many others have used, he said, 'People can read many learned books about the taste of sugar; they can write PhD theses and have endless debates; and they still won't know the taste. But put one little sugar crystal in their mouths and they instantly know it all.'*

Knowing through such direct experience enlivens us by opening our awareness to life energy in its many forms and makes a powerful contribution to our personal wellbeing.

PRINCIPLES OF CENTRING

In addition to the other benefits already discussed, combining the centring and grounding meditations helps us experience and know directly answers to questions such as: 'Who or what am I? Am I my job? Am I my feelings, thoughts, impulses, etc? Am I what I have trained to do? Am I a person? Am I something or nothing?'

The following three principles can help us in our quest for answers to questions like these.

Principle 1: Our energy flows to where our attention goes.
This principle highlights how concentrating our attention on any aspect of ourselves or the world around us builds energy in that.

So, for example, if we want our lives to work out well, the idea is to pay attention to what is working for us. That is, we put energy and intensity into what we want by concentrating on it. Of course, we can also do the opposite. We have already discussed the predictability of these results in the guidelines in Chapter 6.

Principle 2: We are centred where our energies are most concentrated.
This second principle is to do with our sense of self. Think of the examples of this already mentioned (in Chapter 11). We may be centred in the imbibed opinions of others, in our bodies, in our feelings, in our thinking or personalities, and in I-Am. Wherever we are centred is the most energised aspect of us at that time, and we live everything from there. Maybe you can remember when you became so engrossed in something that you experienced the meaning of your life through it: your children (child rearing), a sport (playing soccer), a new set of ideas (hints for highly successful people), an important cause or approach to life (a special diet, securing the health of the planet), or an innovative way of doing things (a new computer system). Many people easily recognise their centres, though some people need practice to become familiar with the process.

Principle 3: To become centred in something of our choice, centre on it for long enough and with sufficient intensity to energise it until it is more intensely charged than everything else.
This third principle is a combination of the first two and enables us to choose to become centred in anything. This is very useful in our daily lives, because it enables us to take charge of our centring. So, for example, we can choose to pay attention to our hearts in order to flood our systems with the sense of loving and wellbeing that arises naturally as we centre there. To build confidence, we can concentrate on the things in which we excel. When we want something, we can concentrate on having it and so become centred in having it. Of course, all of these examples are reminders of the second principle of goal-setting: 'What we concentrate on is what we get'; except that the principles in this chapter are about how we influence outcomes and less on what outcomes we are seeking (see Chapter 6).

Meditation 1: As a general project, choose something that you are highly motivated to learn and spend at least five minutes a day centring-on this in some way. Make your concentration as intense and as one-pointed as you can. Keep doing this, knowing that each time you do it you are increasingly becoming whatever it is. And notice how you gradually start to understand whatever you have chosen through the new insights that arise in you, seemingly out of nowhere. Keep records in your logbook.

This last principle also enables us to change what we are doing if we discover we are centred in unhelpful ways. We may, for example, notice that we have concentrated on the dismal, self-defeating stories people are sharing with us about a project in which we are mutually engaged. Using this third principle, we can recognise that we have centred-on their stories so much that we are now part of them. We can then immediately divert our attention onto optimistic, self-affirming stories or pictures in order to become part of them.

GENERAL CENTRING

Learning to stay centred as we live is important. *Meditation 3: Centring in Your Sense of Self or Observer* in the last chapter will help you to do that quickly. The following meditation is a more extended version that will expand your practice.

Meditation 2: General Centring.

Step 1: Sit upright. Get yourself grounded and keep paying attention to grounding from time to time throughout the meditation. Do this by noticing the physical sensations in your body, the physical things and events around you, and their sensate connections in you.

Step 2: When you are ready, close your eyes and pay attention to whatever is in your experience. What are you *noticing*?

Step 3: At this point, also become aware that you are aware and notice what in you is aware – notice your observer. You can do this systematically by becoming aware of a particular part of your body or of the world around you, and noticing in you what is looking at it, listening to it, feeling it, tasting it, smelling it, talking about it to yourself, or what is aware of it through direct knowing.

Step 4: As you become aware of your observer, also begin to notice what it is like. What is your sense of self there? (See the last part of Chapter 11 and the early part of this chapter if you need some examples.)

Step 5: After noticing your experience of your observer, make yourself one with it by centring-on it. You can do this in a variety of ways, so do it in whatever way is easiest for you. Generally what works is to keep your attention on it and encourage yourself to blend, align and become one with it.

Step 6(a): If it is tangible, you could imagine you are settling into it, like settling into a comfortable armchair. See yourself in there, seeing the rest of you from there. Listen to everything from there and allow yourself to hear everything from there. Notice the fragrance and essence of your sense of self and sense all fragrances and essences from there. Talk to yourself about your self and about your experience of becoming increasingly at one with it.

Step 6(b): Alternatively, you may find that you need to allow yourself to expand or dissolve in order to align with your observer. Some people experience this as if their bodily and other experiences have to evaporate, as if they are a field of awareness, not a pinpoint or definable shape or thing at all. So if you need to do this, allow yourself to dissolve or to become nothing.

Step 6(c): If little or none of this makes much sense to you, your observer may be beyond space and time and so it could seem irrelevant to try to align with it at all. If this is true of you, allow yourself to embrace and become the wonderful wholeness of being that you are. Maybe your sense of self is already I-Am.

Step 7: Finally, become one with the fundamental nature or essence of whatever your observer is. At the end, make notes in your logbook, including reference to what your observer was like and what you are experiencing after aligning yourself with it.

CENTRING ALL DAY

As we become proficient at unifying with our observers, we find life taking on different qualities, as if something wonderful that we have known forever is increasingly guiding and directing us in our lives. We start to live life, rather than spending our time trying to manage it. It is understandable, then, that learning to stay centred like this all day could make a wonderful difference to us.

Remember, too, that both our ongoing awareness of and oneness with our observer are fundamentally important because they keep the life force flowing into us. Note the necessary part our awareness plays in this. Without the awareness, there is no flow. Fortunately, learning to be centred all day need not add significantly to what we are already doing about grounding. We can do both at the same time.

This means that all the suggestions given for making grounding habitual can be used with centring. So you can simply add centring to what you are doing with grounding (see Chapter 10) and then enjoy the changes in your experience!

Exercise 1: At the end of each day, think back on your day and log those times you experienced a sense of centred-ness in your observer – worldly-ness, body-ness, me-ness, I-ness or I-Am-ness. Note what this was like. Also, make brief notes on what it was like to lose your centre, your 'sense of self', 'awareness that you were aware' or your sense of being 'aligned with the observer' of what you were experiencing.

13
Fulfilling Our Awareness

Inspiration, awareness and aliveness go together. When we have one, we have the others; and we can't have one without the others. So, in order to be fully alive, to be inspiring (breathing in) the Infinite, and to be experiencing personal wellbeing, we need to remain aware of our inner and outer worlds, and their sensate connections. And we need to sustain this awareness.

In fact, our natural state is to be fully aware: to feel what we feel, to see what we see, to hear what we hear, to taste and smell what is there, and to know what we know. We are hardwired for this and it takes far more energy to block awareness than it takes simply to allow it. Access to or being in the Infinite saturates our consciousness with inspiration; that is, with understanding, insight and the answers to questions, with the fulfilment that comes with love, completion and healing, and with much more.

Also, as already discussed, awareness is fundamental to the flow of Life and to our direct experience of it. When we are aware and responsive to what is there, we will experience our aliveness directly and with full intensity. If we inhibit our awareness or responsiveness to it, however, we inevitably inhibit or block its flow through our systems with potentially harmful consequences.

At best, we will have limited our experience of our aliveness and satisfaction. At worst, we may have so inhibited the flow of life force through us that we have become physically, emotionally, mentally or spiritually unwell or unbalanced. We may even die. The origins of these limiting patterns are usually to be found in our upbringings and lifestyles.

Fortunately, grounding and centring are powerful remedies for this. Using them produces rapid improvement for many people, and eventual improvement for virtually everyone. We can watch as people come to life in front of our eyes; hear a new vitality and strength in them; and feel a greater sense of presence when they are around because of the vitality they increasingly radiate.

And we can do more. We can release the contractions that inhibit our natural flow by cultivating our awareness, and we can begin doing this using three related processes. They are *noticing*, *accepting* and *experiencing*. We can cultivate these as we live our day-to-day lives, or by stopping our ordinary activities and meditating specifically on them. Each time we do either, we hone these awareness skills and make ourselves more available to the life force pressing for attention and expression.

NOTICING

Noticing is to do with paying attention, with being aware of what is. Without noticing there is no awareness, for whatever is there and unnoticed doesn't exist for us. So it is important that we notice both whatever is affecting us and what those effects are. We need to stay alert and to cultivate our awareness of every aspect of our experience: our actions, perceptions, thoughts, feelings, memories, impulses, desires, fantasies, knowledge – anything and everything. And we need to notice whatever is occurring inside and around us. To repeat, what we don't notice, we miss, and so to that extent we are not fully present in our lives. Noticing is something that we can practise and cultivate every day, too. So practise being alert and aware in all that you do. It will help to bring you to life.

Meditation 1: Noticing. Do this meditation while standing still, sitting with your eyes closed, or moving around with your eyes open. Whatever method you choose, the goal is simply to observe.

Step 1: If you choose to stand or move, look around you, listen to the sounds around you, touch what is close to you, and notice the fragrance and essence of what is there by smelling and tasting it. Be attentive to each one. If you choose to sit, close your eyes and pay attention to what you are experiencing. As you meditate like this, notice whatever registers in your awareness. Pay close attention to it. Notice any thoughts, feelings, memories, desires, impulses, fantasies or physical sensations. Actively observe different aspects of them; don't simply touch, glimpse or hear them briefly and leave it at that.

Step 2: Also, while noticing, ensure that you include in your awareness the physical sensations that accompany your experiences. This is very important.

Step 3: As you are noticing, also remember to notice that you are noticing. Remember that meditation involves cultivating self-awareness through centring, so the 'noticing that you're noticing aspect' is very important and different from simply noticing. It will help you to become aware of the observer of all you are noticing, or your sense of self (see the previous two chapters for more details). When you finish, make notes in your logbook.

ACCEPTING

Accepting is to do with acknowledging the presence or existence of what is. We don't aim to accept what is there as if it is all right with us, moral, comfortable or the like. We are accepting the reality that it is there, whatever it is. Without this acceptance, we inhibit or distort our awareness of that reality. As with noticing, we can benefit from practising acceptance at every opportunity.

Importantly, as part of this acceptance we welcome, even cherish, whatever we are noticing. We allow it without trying to diminish our awareness, divert it, push it away, suppress it, and without trying to increase or change it in any way. We simply accept the presence of what we are aware of in whatever its form is. We embrace the fact of the presence of what we notice.

This type of acceptance actually depends on something very simple and perhaps surprising. To accept the presence of what we are noticing, we have to accept both *our responses* to its presence and remain *completely open* to whatever is stimulating these responses – whether the stimuli is internal or external. For example, if we feel disturbed by people around us, worried about the future, or delighted with an unexpected event, we notice the fact of our responses and their causes, and we accept both. Relaxation is an important key in this process, because it softens our bodies and helps us to open up to what is there. So, remembering to stay relaxed is often a great help.

Meditation 2: Noticing and Accepting. We now add accepting to the last meditation. As you do this, be aware that accepting is not primarily a cognitive or intellectual process, nor does it involve labelling or categorising, although these approaches may lead you to greater acceptance at times. Accepting is a process of welcoming, opening up to and acknowledging the presence of what we are noticing – and allowing it. There is no need for you to do anything with what you notice other than to accept it. Relax into whatever you are noticing and, if it helps, repeat the words: 'I accept you', 'I accept you are in my awareness' or 'I welcome, acknowledge and accept you are in my awareness.' Record what occurs in your logbook after you finish.

EXPERIENCING

Experiencing takes our awareness to another level. With noticing, we become aware of what is in or around us; with accepting, we open ourselves to welcome and align with the presence of what we notice; with experiencing, we concentrate our attention on the responses we are having and become one with them. As with the other two, we can practise this orientation in our everyday lives.

The primary goal here is to allow our experiences to live in us. They are not simply part of what is occurring inside our awareness anymore; nor are we cultivating a detached awareness of them. They fully become our experiences. Again using relaxation, we allow our bodies to soften, to go quiet, to become transparent, and to open up to our experiences. As we do, those experiences begin naturally to spread into the rest of our bodies. We allow that spreading and accept the experiences that this stimulates.

Meditation 3: Noticing, Accepting and Experiencing. Begin by doing the last meditation. Notice what is in your awareness, whether it is inside or outside your body, and accept whatever you experience as you do. As you accept it, allow and encourage your experiences to spread all through you. To do this, you relax yourself and open yourself to whatever is there. You may also welcome any experiences with, 'I accept you.' Then imagine you are completely immersed in your experiences, saturated by and at one with them. There is no separation; you are now living your experience. When you finish, make notes in your logbook.

SUSTAINING OUR AWARENESS

Given its central place in keeping life energy flowing through our systems, it is clearly important that we learn to sustain our awareness for the everyday benefits this offers us. Many meditations train us to be aware, to sustain that awareness and to cultivate awareness that we are aware (see Chapter 8). Remember, though, that this learning may take repeated practice in order for you to become deeply receptive and available to I-Am. The important thing is to persist. And we can do more.

Meditation 4: Sustained Awareness Day-to-Day. Pay attention during your daily life. If you notice your attention wandering, stay relaxed and gently bring your awareness back to your current task or practice. Persistence is the goal: if you are doing a shopping list, keeping coming back to your list; if you are doing a breathing meditation, keep returning to your breathing; if you are doing your grounding, keep returning to the physical dimensions of your experience; if you are talking to someone, stay attentive to the conversation. Keep recording your experiences in your logbook.

Even if days, weeks, months or years pass before you can routinely experience the concentration this meditation encourages, your persistence will pay off. And celebrate your small or large gains, because every one of them is increasing your aliveness and your wellbeing, also your potential availability to I-Am.

To help more specifically, here is a list of approaches to deal with wandering attention:

- Allow your attention to float around and notice that you are.
- Know that awareness that you are aware is self-awareness.
- Understand that the primary goal is to stay with your moment-by-moment experiences.
- Practise welcoming what is in your awareness without trying to do anything with it.
- Name your experiences specifically: 'hot belly', 'feeling angry', 'thinking about my children', 'remembering the holiday', 'noticing car noise in the street', etc.
- Name your experiences generally: 'body sensations', 'feelings', 'thoughts', 'memories', 'outside event', etc.

Remember that grounding and centring remain fundamentally important throughout. We want our primary attention to include our sensate experiences of the inside and outside, whatever else we are doing, and we want to align with the observer.

In all of this, as we heighten the sensate in our experiences of ourselves and our worlds, we encourage our availability and full knowing of I-Am and the Infinite. Our bodies are the key to this availability and knowing – the 'royal road' to awakening and enlightenment. Understanding this is very important.

Meditation 5: Grounding, Centring and Naming. Start this meditation by doing *Meditation 4*. After doing this for several minutes, ground yourself fully by cultivating your physical awareness of your sensations, the world around you, and their sensate connections. At the same time, cultivate your awareness that you are aware and align with your sense of self while doing this. When it occurs to you to do it, name your experiences (generally or specifically). Record in your logbook how well this helps or doesn't help you to sustain your awareness.

14
Nourishing Our Bodies

During the early 1980s, Elizabeth and I started an informal research project into the influence of dietary habits on personal wellbeing. We had observed a possible connection between eating patterns and how people were managing their lives. In particular, we were interested in any balance or imbalance between what they were eating and their activity levels during a normal 24-hour day.

Accordingly, we asked everyone two simple questions:

1. *On average, what do you eat for breakfast, lunch and your evening meal each day?*
2. *On average, how active are you in the morning, afternoon, evening and night?*

The results were extraordinarily consistent, particularly given that we were seeing people from a wide range of backgrounds and in different countries, most of whom were consulting us for help to improve their lives. Some of them were seriously troubled. By the end of our enquiries, we had responses from between 900 to 1,000 people.

Three main patterns emerged:

1. *Only about 1 in 20 people were eating three meals a day, and mostly they ate their largest meal at night.*
2. *Only about 1 in 40 people were eating three meals a day that were balanced with their activity levels.*
3. *Those eating three meals a day were generally happier and more at ease than those who didn't; and the 1 in 40 who balanced their food intake with their activity levels as well were doing much better than those who didn't.*

These patterns prompted us to make several specific suggestions to our clients about dietary balance (see Chapter 15). Our goal was to help people to eat and drink so that their nutrient and energy intakes were in balance with their daily and nightly activity levels.

The outcomes[27] were remarkable: everyone who started to eat as recommended by us found that an estimated 60% to 95%

of all their emotional and psychological problems simply dissolved with no other intervention!

We were initially astonished by this result. These percentages are huge. However, we soon realised that our bodies, as the physical platforms of all our experience are fundamental to our wellbeing. When our bodies are in balance, they draw all of our experiences towards that same kind of balance; and when they are out of balance, whatever the reasons, they draw all of our experiences towards the same kind of imbalance. We understood that this was why helping people to maintain nutritional balance promoted emotional and psychologically balance, too. Some also noticed a difference in their availability to spiritual nourishment. (Other physical needs are discussed in Chapters 16 and 17.)

Exercise 1: Eating and Activity Patterns. For the next three days, note briefly in your logbook what and how much you eat for your breakfast, lunch, evening meal, and in any snacks. Also, summarise your activity levels throughout the day and night. For example, 'busiest in afternoon', 'heavy physical work in morning', 'sitting around at night', 'sleeping from 11.00pm', or 'still at work and very active late into the night, slept in afternoon, only did a little in the morning.' We will return to these notes.

FOOD AS FUEL FOR LIFE

What we eat and drink is fundamental to our survival and general wellbeing. People who have well-balanced diets stay physically healthier, emotionally more balanced and happier, think more clearly, and are more alert. Also, their bodies are more receptive to life energy because of their greater vitality and aliveness than when they don't eat well. And you can discover the truth of these assertions for yourself. These patterns arise from two realities.

1. Food and water are necessary for survival. The ingredients that make up our bodies come largely from what we eat and drink. When we don't get sufficient food for an extended period we suffer from malnutrition, our bodies break down and eventually stop working altogether. Also, our bodies are substantially made of water, which has to be kept at the right level for many crucial bodily processes to keep working well. Drinking water without additives every day is therefore important. We need to be aware that, while there are benefits from drinking tea, coffee and alcohol, they are dehydrating, which needs to be compensated for if we drink a lot of them.

2. Food and drink provide fuel for our bodies and without that fuel our bodies stop working. One of the most useful ways of thinking of food and drink is as fuel. Like our cars, which don't run unless they have fuel in the tank, we need fuel in our digestive systems to keep going. However, there is one interesting difference between cars and bodies. Our bodies are designed to draw fuel from inside themselves – from stored fat and other body tissues – when the readily available food in them runs out. So, in this sense, we have a reserve tank. However, unlike a car with a reserve tank, when our bodies switch to their reserves, there is an immediate and often significant drop in performance. For example, children who don't eat breakfast often have difficulty concentrating at school in the morning.

This performance change occurs because the process of releasing the stored energy into our bodies also takes energy. So, as well as the energy we are expending to do whatever we are doing, we need to use still more energy to release what we need for those activities.

Exercise 2: Running Low on Fuel. Think briefly about the last few weeks or months. Remember times when you had not eaten for an extended period during the day. Record in your logbook what you noticed. In particular, were you aware of finding it harder to concentrate or to do things than when you had eaten a relatively short time before?

FOOD FOR THOUGHT

Dietary knowledge is expanding all the time. Also, taking expert advice if we are in doubt about our current eating habits is useful. Much is now known about what foods and drinks contribute to wellbeing and good health, and what contributes to ill health. Unfortunately, experts often disagree and it is not always clear what to do: what was thought to promote health and wellbeing yesterday may be thought to create avoidable problems today.

But watch this space. A relatively new field called nutritional medicine is offering us increasingly sophisticated understandings of the health implications of what we eat. It also tells us how using selective nutrition for treating physical health problems can be helpful. A good example of this is the now well-established discovery of the value of low fat diets in promoting good health and avoiding many physical problems, including heart disease. ('Low fat' doesn't mean 'no fat', for we still need ingredients such as Omega 9 and 3 oils.) Nutritional interventions are also used to promote health by supplying the correct balance of nutrients: the food, antioxidants, minerals and other nutrients our bodies need; and to promote recovery from disease by using an appropriate balance of food and nutritional supplements to target selected organ systems.

Also, in recent times, nutritional medicine has been expanding its understanding of how to influence 'chains' of metabolic processes and is applying this knowledge to people with various physical, emotional, psychological and mental problems, and with promising results.

Advice to you on the particular food you eat, except in the general terms outlined in the next chapter, is not included in this book. Nevertheless, if you think the connections reported below are worth investigating, several books may be worth consulting. They have general information and summaries of many research projects. The discussions and conclusions they contain describe observed connections between common dietary patterns and illnesses such as cancer, heart disease, stroke, multiple sclerosis, obesity, diabetes, osteoporosis, dementia and others.

The suggestions that may be worth your attention are as follows.

Animal-based diets have increasingly emerged as responsible for or major contributors to such diseases. Given those findings, it is hardly surprising that plant-based diets, including non-dairy diets, are seen by some as supporting health and as avoiding or minimising the emergence of many diseases. *The China Project*[28] is well worth reading from this general point of view. It highlights general patterns and gives specific advice.

Your Life in Your Hands[29] deals with breast cancer, mentions prostate cancer, and strongly recommends dairy-free diets for minimising risk and as helpful support when used alongside medical treatment.

Taking Control of Multiple Sclerosis[30] similarly suggests the use of plant-based diets (with the careful inclusion of Omega 3 oils in capsule form, or from eating oily fish) along with other medical therapies as indicated.

Sweet Poison[31] suggests that sugar is addictive, that the body converts sugars into fat, and that current levels of consumption in many parts of the world are associated with the high incidence of obesity, diabetes, coronary and other diseases.

FEEDING ON THE SUN

We also need sunlight to survive. Maybe this isn't as obvious as it used to be because of the now well-established links between melanoma and over-exposure to sunlight, and the public emphasis on these consequences. However, it remains true. This should be obvious because sunlight is a necessary ingredient in the growth of all life on the planet. Without sun, we have no food; and without food, there is no life.

But there is more to it than this. Sunlight is necessary for the creation of Vitamin D by the body. And low Vitamin D levels in people have been associated with a long list of serious physical problems: rickets, muscle weakness, osteoporosis, poor immune system function, hypertension, cancer, MS, Type 1 diabetes, obesity, depression, chronic pain, neurological problems and osteoarthritis. It has also been associated with an increased risk of breast cancer, and cardiovascular events (heart attack, heart failure, or stroke).

People's Vitamin D levels increase when they sun themselves, when they take vitamin D supplements or both. And there are increasing indications that doing these things lowers the risks associated with the above list of diseases.

Without wanting to minimise the danger of getting skin cancer from over-exposure to the sun or sunbeds, some direct exposure to the sun makes far more sense than having none. In fact, the above health implications would indicate that conservative, direct sunning is a mandatory health practice, but for only short periods.

In addition, the sun offers us much more than Vitamin D. Sunlight feeds our bodies with light and heat, and basking in it stimulates a unique kind of fulfilment. Also, it is well known that a depressive illness, called Seasonal Affective Disorder, is more frequent during the long winters in countries near the North Pole and is associated with the absence of sunlight in those places. As time passes, I feel sure we will discover other benefits from sunning ourselves sensibly.

Exercise 3: Sun Time. Note in your logbook how much time you spend with your skin exposed to direct sunlight during spring, summer, winter and autumn/fall. Just noting your general impressions in your logbook will be enough.

15
Balancing Our Diets

Many of the people in our research ate little or no breakfast, only a small amount or nothing at all for lunch, and a large evening meal. This meant their bodies needed food for the majority of their waking hours, and that they were in a 'nutritional state of emergency' – living off their stored energy supplies – for most of the day. No wonder the differences were so great in how well, happy and contented they felt when they started to eat in a balanced way. Interestingly, many of them were not aware of feeling hungry or thirsty because they had been living like this for years and had stopped noticing their hunger and thirst (see Chapter 4).

We need food, water, antioxidants, minerals and sunlight to remain well and healthy. We also need our nutrition in proportion to our activity levels, both overall and specifically in relation to when we are active and inactive. Our experience indicates that life is easier if we have food 'in our bellies' to fuel our bodies during what we are already doing and are about to do. The following five simple principles can help guide us in how to do this.

Principle 1: Eat and drink shortly before and during the active periods of our days.

By doing this, we ensure that we have food and water available in our bodies for immediate use. They will then not need to engage in the energy-costly process of moving what they require from storage. Instead, everything we do will be efficiently energised by the food in our digestive systems. So, instead of living in a nutritional state of emergency, in which the body has to 'eat' itself to keep going, we live in a state of nutritional abundance.

Interestingly, our long experience with undernourished and emotionally unhappy people led us to conclude that people's feelings and thoughts generally matched their physical craving to fill up from the outside. For example, hungry people often feel others should do something for them (feed them) and become preoccupied with how they are being ignored (starved for affection).

A good meal frequently gives temporary relief from these kinds of feelings and thoughts, although any non-nutritional reasons for unhappiness still need to be dealt with in other ways.[32]

Exercise 1: Eating Before and During Activity. Give some thought to what you will be doing tomorrow. Make sure you pay attention to how physically active you will be at different times. Then plan your breakfast, lunch and evening meal so you are nutritionally supplied before or during your active times. Record what you plan to do in your logbook. At the end of the day, briefly review any differences you observed in your energy levels, ability to concentrate, or your sense of wellbeing.

Principle 2: Eat and drink something about every four hours.
Four hours is a long time between meals. Most nutritional value is drawn from what we have eaten or drunk in that time. In other words, the fuel tank will be getting close to empty after that, so wholly or partially filling up again before we run out is important. For an average person, this would mean having breakfast, a mid-morning snack, lunch, a mid-afternoon snack, and then an evening meal. This pattern will keep us well supplied and help us to avoid living an unnecessarily hungry or thirsty life.

Exercise 2: Four-Hourly Intake. Do you have long, active periods during the day when you don't eat and drink beforehand or at the time? If you do, experiment with having at least a snack before or while you are busy, and notice what a difference it makes to you. Record the results in your logbook.

Principle 3: Balance overall food and drink intake with overall activity levels and metabolism.
Three guidelines can help here. First, if you are maintaining a healthy weight, you are adequately supplying your energy needs. Second, if you are putting on weight, you are oversupplying yourself with energy. Third, if you are losing weight, you are undersupplying yourself with energy. (Check with your doctor/physician if you think something else might be contributing to any weight gain or loss.)

Clearly, we also need to know our optimal weights. So if you don't know this, given your height and body frame, consult your doctor/physician or a dietician. An external, objective assessment is often helpful because for many of us this area is emotionally highly charged.

Exercise 3: Overall Food/Drink Intake. Think about the total amount of food you eat in your average day. Note in your logbook whether your weight is stable, reducing or increasing. Also, do you think or feel you are overweight, just right, or underweight? If not 'just right', consider what you could do about it. Get expert advice if you are unsure.

Principle 4: Balance the amount eaten at different times of the day and night with activity levels at those times.
When we are very active, our bodies need a lot of fuel. When they are less active, they need less. For optimal physical and personal wellbeing we need to balance our intake in this way. Think of two patterns as examples. First, consider someone whose day is most active in the mornings and afternoons, and least active in the evenings. This person needs to eat more for breakfast and lunch than for the evening meal, and have a suitable mid-morning and mid-afternoon snack. Second, consider someone whose afternoons and evenings are much more active than their mornings. This person needs to eat lightly in the morning and have more substantial meals for lunch and dinner, plus a good mid-afternoon snack and either nothing mid-morning or only a small snack.

> *A young man who had frequent migraines and episodes of anxiety consulted us after trying unsuccessfully for years to solve the problem. His job involved lifting heavy bags of fruit and vegetables in a local market. He started at 2.30am and finished in the late morning. On work days he was in bed at about 4.00 to 5.00pm. Upon waking for work at 12.30am, he had a cup of coffee. His breakfast was fruit, toast and more coffee at about 7.00am; lunch was two sandwiches, or some sushi, and more coffee at midday; and he had a large dinner of meat and vegetables, a fruit pie or fruit and ice-cream for dessert, and another cup of coffee.*
>
> *His food and drink intake was obviously mismatched with his activity levels. His migraines and anxiety cleared up quickly as soon as he started to eat a large breakfast before leaving home for his early morning heavy-lifting job, a snack of a piece of fruit at about 4.30am, a medium-sized lunch at 6.30am, and a light dinner at 12.00 to 1.00pm.*

Exercise 4: Matching Food/Drink Quantities with Activity Levels. Make a note in your logbook of the general activity pattern of your days and nights. Then think about when and how much you need to eat and drink throughout your days and nights to balance your fuel intake with those activities. Do something to correct any mismatches you discover.

Principle 5: Select what is eaten and drunk according to the body's need for specific nutrients and for important healing ingredients.[33] Our bodies need many inputs, including proteins, carbohydrates, fats and oils, antioxidants, minerals, fibre, and water. It is beyond the scope of this book to go into detailed suggestions to ensure you are getting all the necessary nutrients. These days, there is a wealth of information and expert advice available, and you can take advantage of this if you have any doubts.

CHANGING OUR PATTERNS

After applying the five principles in our lives for a time, we are likely to begin experiencing good energy levels and an enhanced sense of wellbeing. We may be pleasantly surprised at the extent of the changes we notice; for example, when our eating and drinking habits are balanced with our actual bodily needs, many discomforts and problems in other areas of our lives can simply dissolve.

Even so, while the gains are great, making changes in eating patterns can be very challenging. The following suggestions have been helpful to a lot of people:

1. Make the changes a little at a time. Avoid big steps. For example, if you don't usually eat breakfast, start off with small amounts and gradually increase them over a few weeks.
2. In the beginning, if you haven't been eating at particular times that you identify as important, it is often easier to swallow liquid or mashed foods than solid food that you need to chew.
3. Start to notice when you are hungry or thirsty. Eat or drink something soon after you do. (As you decide what to do, remember the principles related to weight gain or loss.)
4. Keep brief notes in your logbook each day about the changes you make and how you are feeling.
5. Talk to someone who can help with ideas about different food and drink so you can make your meals attractive and interesting.
6. Regularly checking in with or reporting to someone else is a good way to persist with helpful changes. Knowing you will have contact with this person can act as motivation for you to stay committed to your program.

16
Resting

Rest helps us to remain physically and emotionally resilient, balanced, alert, refreshed and healthy. To experience its health-giving and sustaining results, we need to make sure our plans include it. This is crucial these days when many of us are so busy.

There are three important aspects to resting that contribute differently to our wellbeing. First, we need to sleep regularly. This recharges and revitalises us after our previous activity and it prepares us for what is to follow. During sleep, we process and resolve the past emotionally, partly through our dreams as well. This helps us to stay mentally balanced and healthy. We also need to sleep long enough to do this, longer than many people think is necessary these days. Second, we need to learn how to relax quickly while on the go in order to release our tensions and pent-up energies. Third, we need to learn to live relaxed lifestyles.

SLEEPING

Many factors influence how much and how well we sleep. Some are constitutional, while others are to do with life's conditions and events. The average adult who is in good health will sleep about seven to eight hours a day. The average child tends to sleep more than this. Also, in our later years we seem to need less sleep. All the same, there are many different patterns, so yours may be different and still be adequate for you. For example, some people sleep so little that they can do two jobs to occupy their waking hours; while others sleep for significantly longer than the average.

Variations also occur due to the effects of events or changes in our lives; for example, the arrival of a baby, becoming ill, having an accident, or having to deal with heavy work or study demands.

Exercise 1: Sleeping Patterns. For the next three days, keep note of the time you go to bed and the time you get up each day. Do you sleep for most of the time you are in bed? Add to this any times you took a 'power nap' in addition to your main sleep period. Add up the total for each day. Use something like the table at the end of Chapter 17 to log your usual patterns.

Attitudes and expectations are also extremely important. They greatly influence or determine our sleeping patterns. They can 'put us to sleep', 'keep us awake', 'make us sleep well', 'make us sleep poorly' or 'ensure that we feel fresh (or tired) when we awaken'. Remember: what we concentrate on is what we get. Fortunately, we can change our attitudes, if ours are unhelpful.

Exercise 2: Attitudes to Sleeping. As you lie down to sleep, relax and imagine yourself sleeping and waking up the way you would prefer. We are very suggestible when we are starting to slip into sleep, so we can use this time for some programming or reprogramming. For example, imagine the time you will wake up and that you have woken up after a restful, restorative sleep feeling fresh and ready to get up and enjoy the day/night. You can create an affirmation along these lines to repeat to yourself before sleeping. Similarly, as you get out of bed, affirm that you will feel fresh and alive throughout your day/night. Make a habit of these practices. Keep notes of your progress in your logbook. (The *Creative Release Meditation*[34] can help speed up attitudinal changes.)

The following three general principles can help us to decide how much to sleep and how to establish balanced sleeping habits. Naturally, if we are unwell, or there are other reasons for our sleeping less or more than suggested, we need to get advice, act sensibly and do what is necessary.

Principle 1: On average, sleep and rest in bed until we wake naturally, feel refreshed and have a definite inclination to start our days.
We may need to reorganise the times we go to bed and get up to achieve this. Also, there are clearly periods in our lives when this is not practical, such as when we have young children to care for, or a temporarily demanding work schedule.

Principle 2: Stay in bed for a maximum of about eight hours at a stretch, then get up. If more sleep or concentrated rest than this is needed, take time to sit or lie down later in the day for the extra time that is needed.
Too much time without physically moving can create its own problems, some of which are mentioned in Chapter 17.

Principle 3: Go to bed before 11.00pm and, if possible, have a fifteen-minute power nap between 11.00am and 1.00pm.
These are particularly refreshing and healing times to rest. Our

bodies respond well when we make a practice of sleeping then. Shift workers may need to devise a different schedule.

Exercise 3: Waking Naturally. If you think it would be helpful, plan how you can alter your day and the demands made on you so that you can wake up naturally and get up when you are ready. Make notes in your logbook about the differences you notice when you do this. If you are having difficulty falling asleep, or relaxing well while asleep, you may find the *Relaxation Meditation*[35] helps.

RELAXATION

Relaxation is a natural bodily state that, like other bodily states, influences our feelings and thoughts directly. When relaxed, we feel balanced, at ease, confident and resilient in everything we do. This makes life easier and more fulfilling. Relaxation is important for promoting healing and helping our bodies recover after exercise. It is also important when we are stressed and need a way of releasing our built-up tensions that allows our bodies to return to their normal relaxed states.

Relaxation Procedures

Two approaches to relaxation can help us in most situations: *stationary* relaxation and *active* relaxation.

Stationary Relaxation

The most direct way to relax our bodies is to stop what we are doing for a while and let our muscles go loose. People who practise this become very good at taking short relaxation breaks, perhaps only for a few minutes at a time, that quickly become opportunities to recharge. Having a specific technique for doing this is valuable.

Exercise 4: Relaxation Recording. Obtain a good, short relaxation recording. The *Relaxation Meditation* recording we use has a half-hour track that is ideal for this. Notice your experience before, during and after you use it. And make notes in your logbook. The more often you use a recording like this, the more you are likely to be able to go through the process without it. There is also a self-induced method that anyone can use immediately (see *Exercise 5*).

Exercise 5: Self-Induced Stationary Relaxation. Decide how long you are going to relax (one, five, ten, fifteen … minutes) and have some way of bringing yourself back at the end: a timer, for example. Then take the following steps:

1. Sit up or lie down so that you are fully supported.
2. Notice the contact of your body with what is supporting you and keep bringing your attention back to that contact.
3. Relax deliberately with each outward breath.
4. Increasingly pay attention to the parts of your body that are already relaxed, or more relaxed than other parts.
5. At some time after you stop, make brief notes in your logbook of any welcome changes in how you feel.

Active Relaxation

Although the deepest relaxation is experienced while we are fully supported and inactive, there are ways of relaxing while on the move. One way is to use grounding (see Chapters 9 and 10). You may already have used this and noticed how relaxed you are after becoming grounded.

Exercise 6: Active Relaxation Using Grounding. When you are feeling highly charged, and not relaxed, or have the need to let go, use grounding. Notice your experiences before, during and afterwards. Log the results you get.

In fact, some people find that using grounding is a much easier way to relax than trying to relax directly.[36] Some of us are just not at ease with letting go, sinking away inside, dissolving, or becoming inwardly transparent and quiet in the ways that stationary approaches encourage. Once you become accustomed to relaxing actively, however, you may find that stationary relaxation also becomes easy.

Exercise 7: Self-Induced Active Relaxation. This is a brief, self-induced approach to relaxation for when we only have a little time. For a few seconds or minutes, take the following steps:

1. Stay standing and allow your body to be as loose and released as you can, even if only momentarily.
2. Concentrate specifically on grounding by noticing your physical sensations, the physical world around you and the sensate connection between the two; in particular, notice the contact of your feet with what you are standing on.
3. Each time you breathe out actively encourage your body to go as slack and loose as you can.

4. Keep grounding yourself and concentrate your attention on those parts of you that are already relaxed or more relaxed than other parts.
5. Continue until you need to stop. Notice any changes for the better. You may relax a lot in remarkably little time. Use your logbook to record anything you wish to remember.

17
Exercising

Physical exercise is necessary to keep the body alive, healthy and fit. Without movement the body quickly deteriorates, because continual movement is necessary for maintaining so many bodily processes. Amongst other things, movement helps joints to stay lubricated and free of deposits, to return the blood to the heart from our extremities, to clear congestion, toxins and waste material from the blood, to keep muscles strong and healthy, to move food and waste material through the digestive tract, and to strengthen bones and keep them filled with calcium.

Movement also supports recovery from illness, accident, or operations. In addition, it is essential in the development of neural pathways in children as they grow, for the maintenance of neural health in adults, and for rehabilitation after strokes or other nerve damaging experiences. Also, movement stimulates internal organs, helps to release feelings and other energies from the body, reduces confusion while encouraging clear thinking, and promotes intellectual poise. And this is just a short list!

TYPES OF EXERCISE

Four types of exercise are important because each one contributes to our fitness and health in different ways. They are *routine exercise*, *training*, *anaerobic exercise* and *aerobic exercise*.

Routine Exercise

Routine exercise is what we do as a natural accompaniment to our day-to-day activities. This is the bending, stretching, running, walking, lifting, climbing of stairs, and other exercise that we do most days of our lives. The body needs this kind of exercise, so if you spend a lot of time sitting or standing during your normal day, you might need to consider changing what you do in order to support your health.

Training

Training is the exercise, usually repetitive, that is done to build up bodily health, fitness and vitality. When we train, we deliberately set out to produce desirable changes in the structure and functioning of our bodies. Examples include running, swimming, walking, weight training and cycling. You also might engage in training in a less formal sense through deliberately doing things that help your body, such as climbing stairs instead of using elevators, or when sitting, swinging your legs to keep your knee joints loose and mobile.

Anaerobic Exercise

Anaerobic exercise – so called, exercise without oxygen – relies on stored energy that does not require oxygen to be released. Most routine exercise is anaerobic, since it does not raise our respiration or heart rates significantly. When short bursts of energy are required to fuel the body, such as walking or sprinting a short distance, the exercise can also be anaerobic when it requires little or no sustained oxygen. Most forms of yoga, tai chi and qigong are anaerobic.

Aerobic Exercise

Aerobic exercise – so called, exercise with oxygen – involves extended activity that forces the heart and lungs to work harder in order to make more oxygen available to the body. We know we are engaged in aerobic exercise when our breathing and heart rates go up. Aerobic exercise increases bodily stamina, and because the heart and lungs are involved in the process, they are also exercised and benefit just as the rest of the body does with increased strength, stamina and release from toxins and waste material.

HOW MUCH EXERCISE?

Seventy to one hundred years ago, our lifestyles involved lots of physical activity and our routine exercise provided most of what we needed on a regular basis. However, these days many people live much more stationary lives. So we need to plan exercise periods to ensure we have enough. Naturally the question arises: How do we know how much exercise we need? Four basic principles can help us answer this.

Principle 1: Have at least one to three hours of exercise a day. Aim at more!

This would include both routine exercise and training. Some people do this every day, while others find this a lot even just to contemplate. If you need a substantial increase in the time you are active to meet this suggested level, then the benefits from doing so are likely to be very great and well worth the temporary discomfort that might be involved.

Principle 2: For at least 30 minutes to one hour every day, engage in whole body movement. Aim at more here too!
This is very important, because much of what we do has very local effects on our bodies. We need to ensure that the whole body is exercised. Examples are bending, reaching up, stretching, squatting and walking with upper body involvement. In fact, many household chores are good exercise in this sense.

Specific exercise programs are useful in the modern world for helping people with this, too. For example, hatha yoga, tai chi, qigong and training programs in gyms all have the kind of complete body involvement that is helpful. Log your results.

Principle 3: Have regular aerobic exercise.
Do this at least three times a week for about 30 or more minutes at a time. Walking vigorously is good for a lot of people, and there are many more strenuous approaches. When selecting what we do in this area, we need to take care of our bodies and only do what is good for them. Also, ensure that we do not over-exercise as a general pattern; too much exercise can damage the body.

Principle 4: Before doing anything differently, take into account your current health and fitness, current lifestyle and specific physical needs.
It is important that we respect our current conditions and act in ways that support increasing health and wellbeing; and that we make any changes to our programs gradually, so our bodies have a chance to adapt to what we are doing. Also, persisting will teach us that the results are well worth any effort involved.

Exercise 1: Exercise Patterns and Times. Use something like the Sleep and Exercise Table on the next page to help you to identify how much exercise you are doing each day. Also, you can use the suggested letters to identify the nature of your exercise. ('R' is routine exercise, 'T' is training, 'An' is anaerobic exercise and 'A' is aerobic exercise.) Think about the patterns this reveals and plan how you could modify what you are doing to further support your bodily health. Make notes in your logbook.

☐Mon ☐Tue ☐Wed ☐Thu ☐Fri ☐Sat ☐Sun

While completing your schedule, remember to use the different letters (R, T, An and A) to represent the different type of exercise: routine, training, anaerobic and aerobic.

TIME	SLEEP	EXERCISE
2.00am		
4.00am		
6.00am		
8.00am		
10.00am		
Midday		
2.00pm		
4.00pm		
6.00pm		
8.00pm		
10.00pm		
Midnight		
Total		

Sleep and Exercise Table

Section Three

Harnessing Your Life Energy

18
DISCOVERING THE LIFE IN FEELINGS

Our feelings keep us alive and resilient. Every feeling is important, both the ones we like and those we don't like. As 'emotional blood', they carry vital 'nutrients' that feed our bodies, energy systems and understanding, each feeling contributing something unique. Suppressing them diminishes our vitality, and strong suppression can easily lead to illness or, eventually, death.

They also provide important signals to us about our current reactions to people, situations and events. When flowing freely and integrated with our thinking and our activities, they help us to live with greater ease and balance (see Chapter 19). Feeling them and embracing them as we live makes it possible to have a life rich with pleasure, love, joy, confidence, and fulfilment.

In this chapter we explore how to recognise feelings and emotions, and briefly, how we can increase or reduce their intensity. This is as a prelude to discussing how we can make the most of the advantages feelings offer us in our daily lives.

RECOGNISING FEELINGS

Feelings are more than the physical sensations that they produce in our bodies. They are streams of energy flowing through us, stimulating our sensations and other reactions as they do. To a great extent, we know what and how strongly we feel through these responses. Moreover, it is primarily through the sensations they stimulate that we can best identify what we are feeling.

Here, we will explore three pairs – six basic feelings in all. They are: happiness and sadness, confidence and fear, and love and anger. The pairing is important because each pair uses a distinct channel or circuit in the body that is different from the other pairs. We will consider mixed feelings and emotions later.

Now, while using our sensations is primary in recognising feelings, other aspects can also help.[37] The list below is a summary of these. Different feelings:

- have characteristic types of stimuli or causes;
- cause distinct sensations in the body;
- have characteristic energy flowing through the body;

- influence the sound and production of the voice;
- lead to different types of behaviour;
- incline us to certain kinds of thinking; and
- invite different sorts of responses from others.

HAPPINESS AND SADNESS

Happiness

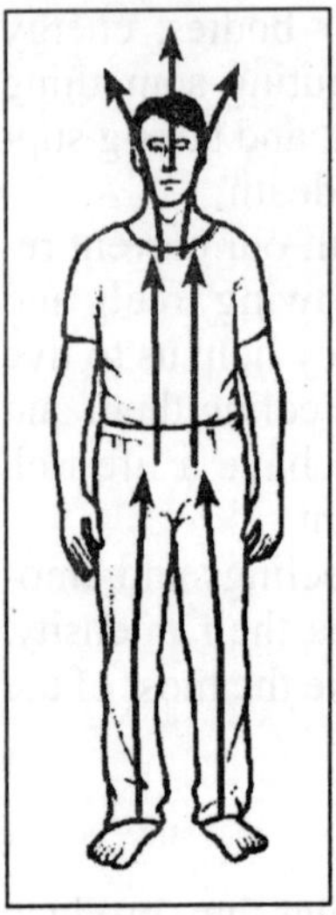

Stimuli: Getting something we want or like; or perceiving something that balances the inside and outside as it uplifts the spirit.

Sensations: Soft, resilient, light, warm, radiant, bubbling, uplifting. Relaxed and balanced muscle tone.

Energy Flow: Flooding or bubbling up through the midline from feet to head and out the top.

Voice Sound: Shrill with excitement, often-high pitched.

Spontaneous Behaviour: Laughing, smiling, giggling, jumping up and down, shouting gleefully, clapping hands happily.

Thinking: Free, open, frivolous, relaxed.

Common Responses from Others; Happy, joyous sharing; joining in the fun, wanting to be involved.

Exercise 1: Feeling Happy. Record in your logbook what you and others you know do and experience when feeling happy. Are there any major differences between your experience and the above description?

Sadness

Stimuli: Loss or anticipated loss of someone, some thing, hopes, dreams, attitudes, expectations, etc that are important to us.

Sensations: Soft, wet, dark, disturbed, warm to hot rising energy that may cause constriction/discomfort/pain in the diaphragm, throat, eyes, etc.

Energy Flow: Energy rising from the pelvic floor, up through the midline and out of the head causing convulsive contractions of the diaphragm.

Voice Sound: Wailing, hesitant, mixed with crying or sobbing,

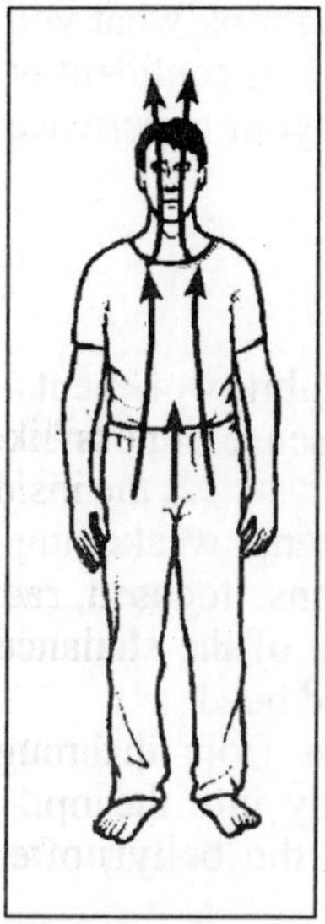

deep or high-pitched depending on where the sadness is centred (the higher up the body, the higher the voice pitch).

Spontaneous Behaviour: Curling over, crying, sobbing, reaching out for nurturing contact, tears, running nose, and saliva often copious.

Thinking: Concentrated on loss, missing, being left out or left behind, or on how to replace the lost person, creature, thing, etc.

Common Responses from Others: Offer nurturing or succour.

Exercise 2: Feeling Sad. Record in your logbook what you and others you know do and experience when feeling sad. Are there any major differences between your experience and the above description?

CONFIDENCE AND FEAR

Confidence (also known as security)

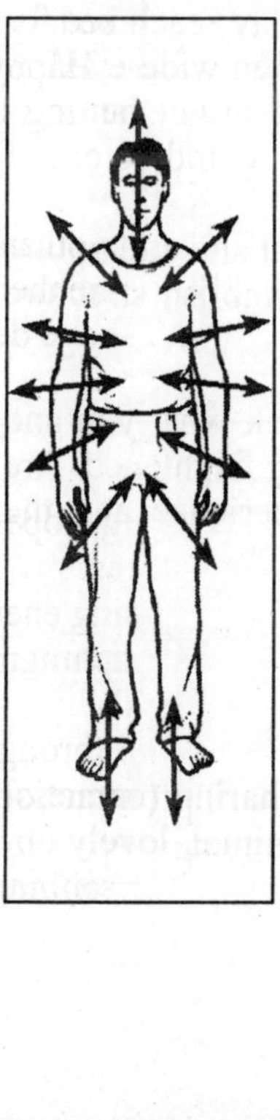

Stimuli: The perceived predictability and stability of events and the perceived ability to cope with them; the presence of some sort of reliable structure.

Sensations: Open, easy, relaxed, quiet, 'nothing', transparent, balanced.

Energy Flow: Energy is in a state of balance, complete openness of inside to outside and outside to inside, no flow, only grounded and centred presence.

Voice Sound: Open, clear, balanced, relaxed, even.

Spontaneous Behaviour: Balanced and open manner, available to others and self-revelatory, paying attention and responsive to the present.

Thinking: Focussed on the I-Am-here-and-now; demonstrates awareness of themselves, other people and their context; balanced.

Common Responses from Others: Making themselves available; easy, open responses.

Exercise 3: Feeling Confident. Record in your logbook what you and others you know do and experience when feeling confident or secure. Are there any major differences between your experience and the above description?

Fear

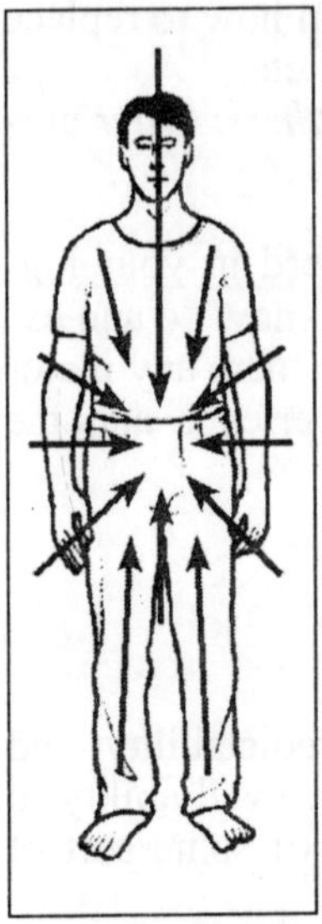

Stimuli: Perceived unpredictability of events, doubt in ability to cope, and a sense of possible risk or harm; loss of structure.

Sensations: Cold to frozen, weakening, sometimes dizzying; sensations focused inwards and flooding into the pit of the stomach or belly from the arms, legs and head.

Energy Flow: Energy flows from the outside and the edges of the body into the midline (possibly strongest from the belly up to the heart).

Voice Sound: High-pitched, shrill, panting or breathless, perhaps crying out or screaming.

Spontaneous Behaviour: Fleeing, freezing, withdrawing or striking out. May reach out for support (social or physical), often wide-eyed.

Thinking: Emphasises what might be or is unpredictable, could go wrong, could be out of control, is risky; focussed on potential threats.

Common Responses from Others: Reaching out and attempting to reassure, to protect, to provide support, to establish structure (predictability) and to offer help.

Exercise 4: Feeling Fear. Record in your logbook what you and others you know do and experience when feeling frightened. Are there any major differences between your experience and the above description?

LOVE AND ANGER

Love

Stimuli: Actual or anticipated heart-centred sharing (oneness) with a living organism, thing or place (person, animal, lovely object, sacred site…).

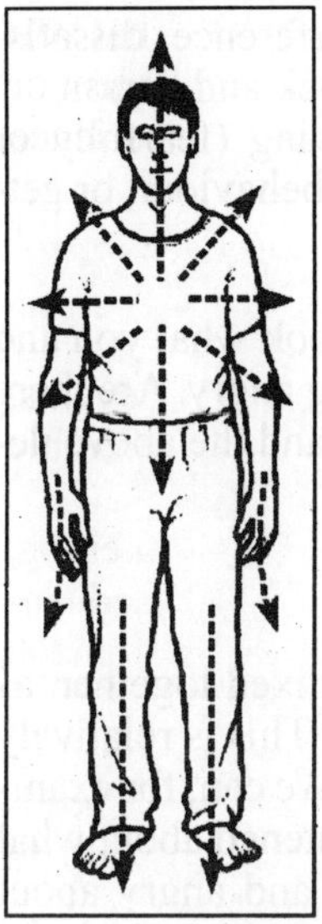

Sensations: Warm, melting, fuzzy looking, mellow sounding, sensations in the heart, limbs and head.

Energy Flow: Energy flows from the heart out through the edges of the body to the outside; warming and melting as it goes.

Voice Sound: Soft, warm, mellow, sweet, tender, intense, 'pink'.

Spontaneous Behaviour: Reaching out to draw into a hug, enfold, and blend; using words, looks and gestures to move closer and to join with others.

Thinking: Centres on mutuality, sharing, co-operation, joining, resolution, caring, mutual respect, and how to act according to these.

Common Responses from Others: Reaching out and reciprocating to the offered joining, blending, sharing and love.

Exercise 5: Feeling Love. Record in your logbook what you and others you know do and experience when feeling loving. Are there any major differences between your experience and the above description?

Anger

Stimuli: Actual or perceived interference or oppression; over-structure in relation to personal activities, aspirations, etc.

Sensations: Hot, hard-muscled, strong, tight, rigid sensations; hardness in everything.

Energy Flow: Energy flows from the heart out through to the edges of the body and then to the outside, hardening and strengthening as it goes.

Voice Sound: Hard, penetrating, strident, strong, shouted, projective, determined.

Spontaneous Behaviour: Striking out, making threats, acting decisively and with strength, creating distance from others, acting to remove interference or oppression, scowling, making fists.

Thinking: About disruption, oppression, interference, dissatisfaction, what isn't working, what is likely to block and harass.

Common Responses from Others: Withdrawing (fearfully or otherwise) and getting out of reach of the angry behaviour, or getting angry back and standing their ground.

Exercise 6: Feeling Anger. Record in your logbook what you and others you know do and experience when feeling angry. Are there any major differences between your experience and the above description?

MIXED FEELINGS

Our feelings rarely come one at a time. When mixed together, as they often are, we need to deal with the mixture. This is relatively easy, because the different feelings are obvious. We can, for example, feel happy/excited about a new job and frightened about what will be expected of us; loving towards a child and angry about what he/she has just done; sad about someone betraying a trust and scared about the impact of this on our future relationship; and confident about the way a project is unfolding and happy about the compliments we are receiving.

Of course, we may also have more than two feelings in the mix: sad at the loss of a loved one, angry at the disruption to our lives, scared about the future without this person, happy (relieved) that this person is suffering no longer, confident that others will offer needed support, and loving in response to the tenderness and caring of good friends. No wonder we say at times: 'I have mixed feelings about that!' Also, no wonder our feelings are such a rich source of aliveness.

Identifying what our feelings are, whether one, two, three or more is an important step in taking care of ourselves and benefiting from the aliveness feelings bring to us in each moment (see Chapter 19).

Exercise 7: Mixed Feelings. Think back over the last few days and identify three times that you had mixed feelings. Note in your logbook what the feelings were and what you were responding to with each.

EMOTIONS

As the word is used here, emotions are a combination of thoughts and feelings: we think something and have feelings about our thoughts. These responses often need to be managed differently from the way we handle single or mixed feelings because thinking adds another dimension. Emotions are recognisable in the interplay between thinking, feelings and bodily sensations.

Examples of emotions are: adequacy – thinking we can cope with something and feeling secure about that; inadequacy – thinking we can't cope with something and feeling frightened about that; wary – concentrating on what could go wrong and feeling frightened about that; passionate – thinking how important something is and feeling happy/loving/angry about that; and embarrassed – thinking about other people noticing us and feeling happy to be noticed but frightened about what will happen now we have been noticed.

Of course, there are many more emotions and we can find out what their ingredients are by following the above pattern: observing our thoughts and our feeling responses to them.

Exercise 8: Identifying Emotions. Consider two or three emotions with which you are familiar and note the thinking and feeling part of them in your logbook. You could choose your own, or use one of the following: self-importance, satisfaction, excitement, guilt, exultation, resentment, concern, defiance, or jealousy.

INCREASING OR DECREASING OUR FEELINGS

Learning to recognise feelings is a wonderful advance because we gain a basic understanding of this very significant aspect of our inner lives. Doing so also enables us to manage our feelings-based reactions and, very importantly, to learn how we can modify or harness these reactions so we are empowered by them rather than feeling as if we are at their mercy (see Chapter 19).

We can harness our feelings because they have distinctive causes. These feeling reactions help us to identify the nature of the situations we are in and think about obvious things we can do to change our responses or the situations themselves. We will briefly consider how to change our responses by using the table below. Notice that what increases the intensity of one feeling in each pair decreases the intensity of the other, and vice-versa.

Exercise 9: Increasing and Decreasing Feeling Intensity. Remember two feeling you have had today. Using the following table, identify what caused them. Then make notes in your logbook about what you could do to increase or decrease those feelings. Think concretely and specifically. Do at least one thing in your notes and notice the results you get. Log those results.

Feeling	Increasing (↑) or Reducing (↓) Intensity
Happiness	↑: Concentrate on happy events; seek pleasure, act to produce balance. ↓: Close down, notice what you don't have, notice imbalance, emphasise dislikes, losses.
Sadness	↑: Concentrate on losses, what will be missed, on pain and distress. ↓: Let go of loss, express feelings, grieve. Seek happiness, balance, or pleasure.
Confidence	↑: Seek openness and structure, feel fully, get grounded. Open to I-Am-here-and-now. ↓: Close down, notice the unpredictable, unmanageable, risky, dangerous.
Fear	↑: Seek rapid change. Notice the unpredict-able, unmanageable, risky, dangerous. ↓: Seek openness and structure, feel fully, get grounded. Open to 'I-Am-here-and-now'
Love	↑: Express love, tenderness and caring. Seek common ground, sharing, oneness, union. ↓: Concentrate on contention, separation, interference, disagreements, division.
Anger	↑: Notice interference and oppression, provoke them. Concentrate on disagreements. ↓: Seek to join and resolve issues, remove obstacles and splits. Express love and caring.

19
LIVING THE ALIVENESS IN FEELINGS

Feelings provide wonderful motive power. They can energise our thinking, guide our understanding towards what is required in many situations, and propel us into action to do what is desirable or necessary. Instead of struggling with them, which a lot of people do, we can learn to notice, accept and experience them (see Chapter 13), and then ride the wave of their aliveness. Two general approaches can help us here: a stepwise approach, which concentrates on goals and outcomes; and a meditative process, which involves centring in expanded awareness.

STEPWISE APPROACH

This systematic way of approaching feelings is based on two assumptions: first, that people prefer to feel happy, confident and loving (compared with sad, frightened and angry); and second, that we can act to encourage ourselves to feel differently without suppressing or diminishing the feelings we are having at the time. We can also expand the benefits and release the obstacles in our current situations by making and acting on deliberate plans.

There are five steps:

1. Identify the feeling or feelings.
2. Discover the cause, which may be 'internal' or 'external'.
3. Decide on the preferred feelings.
4. Plan what to do to produce these results.
5. Do what is required, or organise to have it done.

1. Identify the Feeling(s)

Using the information in the last chapter, you need to identify what you are feeling, remembering that you may have more than one feeling at a time. To make the learning easier at this stage, select only feeling for now.

Exercise 1: What Am I Feeling? Remember a recent incident. Identify what you felt at the time. Note this in your logbook and keep your book with you as you will need it for the next steps. If you are uncertain about what you felt, review the information in the last chapter. Remember that you may have had mixed feelings; if you did, choose only one of them for now.

2. Discover the Cause

What stimulated the feeling you had? Generally, feelings can be stimulated by something going on around us, or a thought, impulse, desire, memory, physical event, etc, inside us. If the cause is not obvious you can use the general information in the table below to help.

Feeling	General Cause
Happiness	Something important that balances inside and outside, or acquiring something we like, have wanted, have worked for …
Sadness	Loss or anticipated loss of a person, thing, attitude, etc that was or is important to us.
Confidence	The perceived predictability or stability of events and of our ability to cope.
Fear	Loss of structure, or perceived unpredictability and inability to cope with events, a sense of impending risk or harm.
Love	Actual or anticipated heart-centred sharing (oneness) with another person, living creature, beautiful object, sacred site...
Anger	Actual or perceived interference or oppression, or over-structure in relation to personal activities and goals.

So, for example, if you feel happy, you identify what you have received that you value, what brings balance to your life; if sad, who has died (gone away…) or what you have lost (mislaid …);

if confident, what is stable and reliable; if frightened, what is unpredictable and risky; if loving, with whom or what have you opened your heart and blended; and if angry, what you experienced as interfering or oppressive in the situation.

Exercise 2: What Caused the Feeling? Take the feeling you identified in the last exercise and identify what caused it. Be specific if you can. Note this in your logbook. There might be several contributing causes.

3. Decide on the Preferred Feelings

Clearly, if you want more of a particular feeling, you simply decide to seek or promote more of the same (see the table in Chapter 18). You can also get significant guidance from the feeling pairs. For example, if you want to stop feeling sad, it is often easiest to promote happiness (the happiness circuits are already opened by the sadness); if fear, promote confidence (fear has opened the confidence circuits); and if anger, promote love (anger has opened the love circuits). Remember to avoid concentrating on 'not sad', 'not scared' or 'not angry', because where you start is where you finish (see Chapter 6).

In fact, even as you begin imagining your preferred feelings, your current feelings will begin to change. For as you imagine feeling happy, confident or loving when you are feeling sad, frightened or angry respectively, your system starts to soften, because the feeling you are imagining is more expansive than the feeling you are having. Then, even if your current feeling intensifies for a while, the happiness, confidence or love that is also intensifying will wash your discomfort from your system and bring new ways of thinking, feeling and responding.

Importantly, handling things in this way enables us to honour the presence of our uncomfortable feelings and use their energies in the process of deciding what we would prefer to feel.

Exercise 3: Conceiving the Feelings You Want. Check your logbook for the feeling you had and think about what you want to feel. If relevant, use the feeling paired with this as a guide. Note what you decide in your logbook.

4. Plan What to Do

These plans are designed so the situations they create will stimulate you to have the feelings you prefer. They are the answer to the question: What needs to be occurring inside or around me so I feel what I want to? Once decided, in relation to your feelings, your goals could be: 'I am feeling happy because (or about) …', 'I am feeling confident because (or about) …' or 'I am feeling loving because (or about) …'

For example, 'I am feeling happy because I have my new car', 'I am feeling confident because I know where I stand with you now' or 'I am feeling loving after sharing the wonderful meal last night.'

The steps involved in the tasks of producing what fills the blanks above (e.g., the new car, the open discussion, and the shared meal) are the plan. The guidelines for goal-setting and clearly defining tasks are helpful here, too (see Chapters 5 and 6).

Exercise 4: Making Plans to Deal with Feelings. Think about what you need to do to change what you are feeling into what you would like to feel. We can often produce both results with the one action. Add your plans to your logbook.

5. Do What is Required

We can use our feelings again with this final step. Their intensity provides motivation and a source of energy for action. To use this intensity, you encourage yourself to keep feeling what is there and, while doing so, you do what is necessary to achieve the goals you have set. Your feelings then act as fuel for your activities.

When we like what we are feeling, this is often easy to do and most people have had this experience. You keep feeling happy, confident and loving as you go about doing what will promote more of the same and the feelings themselves seem to make what you are doing easier.

In fact, while it may seem paradoxical, the same thing works when we are sad, scared or angry. By continuing to feel those feelings and deliberately 'expressing them into' the activities designed to change things for the better, a transformation occurs. Remembering that the purpose is to feel happy, confident or loving is important. The result is that you feel better as a result of your primary intention to improve things and that your discomfort is used to fuel what you do.

For example, while feeling sad, you can use the energy in your sadness to seek or create situations in which you will be happy again; while feeling frightened and seeking security, you use the fear as energy to produce situations in which you feel confident; and while feeling angry and seeking love, tenderness and caring, you use your angry energy to act decisively to produce the changes you want.

We may not say anything specifically about our feelings when doing this; however, we could. Examples of things you might say are:

- While feeling sad: 'I was always happy when we did …', 'I liked the way he/she did …' and 'I used to laugh at …'
- While feeling frightened: 'I can rely on … to take care of this', 'I don't know what'll happen, but I want to feel secure about …' and 'So I feel confident about … will you do …?'
- While feeling angry: 'I want to be able to feel loving and tender with you, and when you do … I don't', 'There is so much we could share and enjoy, and I want you to start doing … so we can' and 'You're really important to me and I want you to do things that bring us together.'

Exercise 5: Fuelling Your Action with Feeling. Having decided what you are going to do in the last exercise, now take the necessary action. And as you do, keep feeling whatever feelings are still current for you by actually imagining you are using them to empower what you do. Make notes in your logbook about the results you get.

With mixed feelings we do whatever suits each feeling, which can seem like a lot. However, with only a little practice we can find that all these steps flow naturally into and support each other. Very soon we can be doing it all automatically.

MEDITATIVE APPROACH

The feelings we have been considering are born of the natural contractions and limitations that are a part of living our everyday lives, even the feelings we like. We particularly experience our discomfort in the forms we do because we perceive our sense of self as not able to handle the forces or events that stimulate what we are feeling. We may also feel caught by those forces in ways that keeps us under their influence. Our perceptions can even make them seem so powerful that they are completely unmanageable or unresponsive to our influence. The result is that we keep ourselves tethered to whatever is acting in or on us, instead of realising how powerful and how capable of releasing ourselves we are.

A wonderful way to deal with this is to expand our sense of self by digesting our feelings and our perceptions of the forces

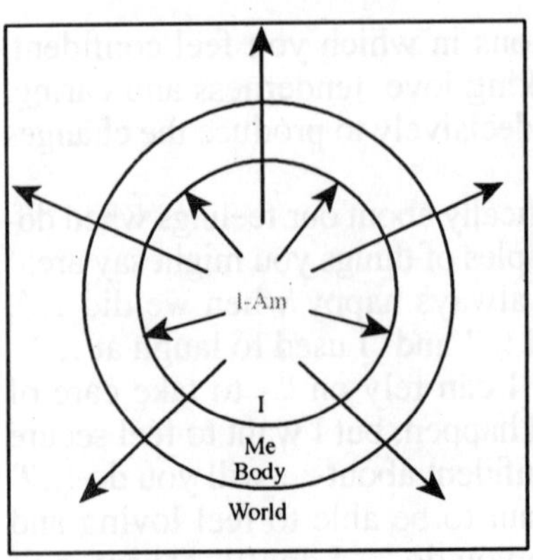

Contraction and Limitation in Worldly Consciousness

at work on or in us. We can do this using a special meditation that involves making ourselves available to all our feelings and perceptions at the times we have them. It prompts a special kind of expansion that increasingly aligns us with and absorbs us in I-Am. The end result is that I-Am becomes our sense of self.

We may start with a fairly dense sense of self (remember self as world, body, me and I) in which there is still contraction and limitation due to our anchoring to our world-bound lives. However, the more available we become to our feelings and perceptions (see Chapter 13), the more we digest these contractions and limitations. Eventually, provided we persist, our sense of self will be the completion, union, oneness and other qualities of I-Am (see Chapter 11). The meditation that follows is a powerful way of approaching this. (You will find other variations of its steps in Chapters 12, 13 and 30.)

Meditation 1: Expanding Our Sense of Self.

Step 1: Opening to Experience. Whatever is going on in you, open yourself to those experiences, including feelings, thoughts, memories and any related aspects such as their causes, relevant people, situations and events. You don't need to process these things, simply allow them to come and go in your awareness in whatever way they do.

Step 2: Notice, Accept and Experience. Notice what these experiences are by being observant; *accept* that they are there without trying to change them, welcoming them as you do and relaxing into their presence; and *experience* their full impact, allowing yourself to know and to live whatever is stimulated. At this stage, as your experiences and knowing unfold, start paying particular attention to the physical aspects of your experience (see Chapter 13).

Step 3: Grounding and Centring. Get well grounded in order to open up to clarity, balance, ease and oneness. When you are grounded, the Infinite digests your contractions and limitations so you increasingly become one with I-Am. Provided you persist, this is a foregone conclusion. Also, the physical, emotional and mental balance that grounding produces makes your participation in I-Am as easy as possible. Centring will flood you with life energy and further support the cleansing of your system as that energy dissolves, refines and transforms your experiences and knowing (see Chapters 9 to 12). Log your observations.

This meditation refines our consciousness, which simultaneously dissolves the confines of our sense of self and makes I-Am and the wonders of the Infinite familiar as self. With this expansion, we progressively realise I-Am, or open to it more, and we discover that our old ways of feeling are transformed. A crucial element is that we primarily centre-on the three sensate dimensions of the grounding, their inner, outer, and linkage parts.

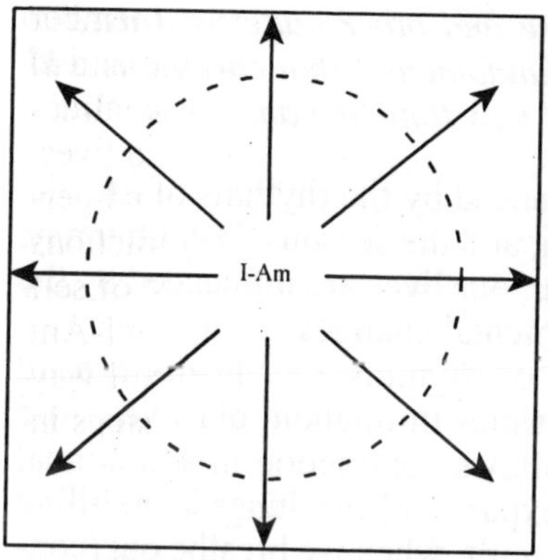

Dissolved Oneness of I-Am and the Infinite

In the end, we become a state of oneness, union and infinite openness to everything. We no longer experience space and time as binding and we are fully realised in the experience and knowing of that. Also, without everyday contraction, feelings take on different qualities from their day-to-day aspects:

Joy – an exquisite happiness – arises from being centred in the I-Am-here-and-now so fully that we have transcended time and space. Being connected to all things, nothing can be lost. Sadness is not possible. Transcendent joy comes from this full balance.

Confidence – a sublime, peaceful, poised certainty – arises from complete openness with and availability to everything. In that infinite state, fear cannot arise, because nothing can seem beyond us or risky. We encompass everything, and there is no structure to lose. Transcendent peace and confidence comes from complete openness.

Love – blissful, ecstatic, sweetness – arises fully in the ultimate union that we experience. Only union is possible and so love is all. Anger simply is not a possibility; because all is one, nothing can interfere with or oppress this infinity. Transcendent love comes from complete union.

20
DAILY CYCLES

I know people who live at full speed and rarely stop, people who rigidly balance activity and rest on a schedule, and others who don't seem to get much done at all. These people only seem to have one style of living. At the same time, I also know people who flexibly adapt to the demands that their lives make on them. While observing these and other patterns, I used to wonder if there is something fundamental that carries us with it, no matter what we do, and I now think the answer is, 'Yes.'

All aspects of our world are influenced by the rhythms of life: the cycles of day and night, the moon, and the seasons. Day after day, month after month, year after year, our lives are influenced by the rhythms of these regular environmental changes.

We also have personal cycles or rhythms. Our hearts expand and contract – many millions of times throughout our lives. And with our breathing, expansion follows contraction in a continual sequence. When we breathe in (expansion) our lungs keep filling with air until they reach a natural limit; when we breathe out (contraction) our lungs expel air until they reach another natural limit. And there are other important cycles as well.

I first noticed one of these patterns when I realised that my energy levels ebbed and flowed in ways I could not easily explain in terms of my needs for sleep, rest and activity. In the summer, particularly, I would wake at dawn and do some of my most creative work until about 9.00am. From then until about 3.00pm I needed to shift to doing routine things. Only after this ended naturally would I feel my creative juices stirring again.

OVERVIEW

After years of investigation, it occurred to me that we participate in a kind of cosmic process, usually without knowing it, a process that breathes our consciousness and life energy in and out of us. More specifically, during the 'in-breath', the centre of our everyday consciousness is carried inwards, streaming away from the world and towards I-Am. When, after a time, the 'out-breath' occurs, the direction reverses and the centre of our everyday consciousness is carried outwards into the world again. Then the cycle repeats.

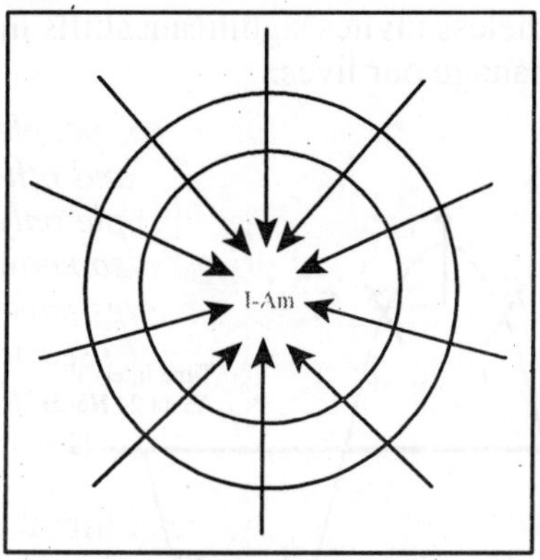

The Infinite Breathing Life Energy from the World into I-Am

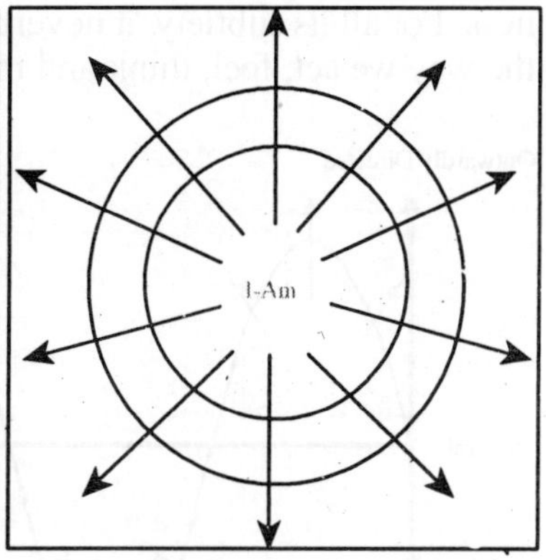

The Infinite Breathing Life Energy into Us and the World through I-Am

HOW THIS WORKS IN EVERYDAY LIFE

Many benefits flow from making ourselves available to this cyclic process; and we can pay a heavy price when we don't adapt what we do according to its phases.

The way these cycles work is similar to the [illegible] our bodies are immersed in air, air that they have to breathe to stay alive and healthy. Our overall systems – bodies, feelings, thinking, personalities, I-Am, etc – are immersed in the Infinite and similarly have to breathe its life energy in and out in order to thrive at every level. To breathe like this, we need to cultivate physical awareness and to align our activities with the three main phases of this cycle.

Consider the following: Are you a morning, afternoon or evening person? Or maybe you are someone who can't get to sleep if you are not in bed by 9.30pm; who stays awake if you are disturbed after 2.00am; who finds it difficult to stay awake in the late afternoon; or someone who falls asleep at about the time you are supposed to get up in the morning. Such patterns are related to this cyclic process.

Exercise 1: Daily Energy Patterns. Do you have any daily patterns similar to these? Make notes in your logbook about them.

For those with the sensitivity to experience this ebb and flow directly in their bodies, it is a subtle streaming, detectable as the faintest of movements, light or sound. It is like the lightest of breezes wafting through every cell in our bodies and consciousness. For all its subtlety, it nevertheless invites significant shifts in the way we act, feel, think and manage our lives.

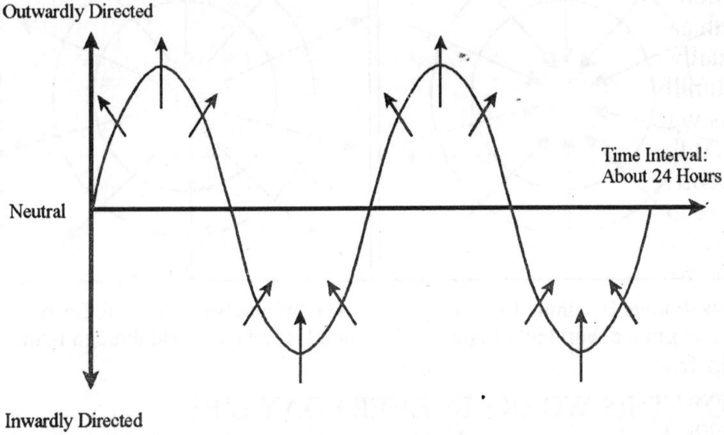

Common Daily Rhythms

Most people seem to complete two full cycles every 24 hours. That is, their life energy moves in and out twice every 24 hours – like two long complete breaths (see the diagram). Not everyone has this pattern though; and you will need to discover what your particular pattern is in order to adapt to it.

HOW TO RECOGNISE YOUR PATTERNS

There are two main ways to identify which phase of your daily cycle you are experiencing: one general and the other specific.

General Method

Our general demeanour, behaviour, attitudes and impulses vary according to which part of our daily cycles we are in. These variations enable us to identify where we are at any given time. To get started, consider the following.

At the height of an *outward phase*: People are usually energetic, vital, alive, alert, quick, extroverted, active and perhaps aggressive. Muscle tone is high and muscles are ready for action. Keeping busy is easy and we tend to thrive on physical activity. Being physically and mentally active is also natural at these times. It is often easier to take the initiative, to make contact with others, and to discharge our responsibilities.

This is a natural time for assertiveness and for making statements, a time for expressing our creativity, innovation and imagination. We may speak in a firm or strong voice, move quickly and with ease, and can look as if we are bubbling with energy. We are usually more alert to the outside than the inside. All of this comes naturally and easily to us during this phase, although usually with less vigour when we are not at the peak.

At the height of an *inward phase*: We are usually inclined to be receptive, contemplative, integrative, slowed down, introverted, more inward looking, quiet, and more inactive. Muscles tend towards relaxation and flaccidity, and are released in readiness for rest. We tend to want to move slowly, take things easily, and perhaps even to stop completely.

We generally find it more congenial to accept initiatives and help from others, to attract people to us, rather than to go out to them. We are more inclined to ask questions than to make statements. We will often speak slowly and quietly, move slowly, and may look de-energised, although it is not a low-energy time. We are usually more alert to the inside than the outside. It is a time for doing routine or ritualistic activities.

At the *transitional times* between the phases: We tend to experience ease, balance, stillness, inner quietness, peacefulness and transparency. It is a pause between our in-breaths and out-breaths; and being balanced like this gives what we have neglected a chance to surface and frees us to take it into account. This surfacing may be uncomfortable if intense feelings are involved, or we don't like feeling directionless, drifty and unmotivated for a while. The flow of our life energy has stopped temporarily and all movement is suspended, which can release us into a deep sense of poise and equanimity with its own unique intensity, provided we embrace the experience.

It is a natural time for evaluating past involvements, identifying loose ends, digesting unfinished business, deciding what to do next and making decisions in a state of balance. We are poised between activity and passivity, between initiative and receptivity, and we can act, think, plan and decide in this state, although we do so differently from when we are in the other two phases.

Exercise 2: Identifying Daily Cycles. Monitor yourself for the next week (or longer if you need to). Identify any patterns in the way you feel, think and act at different times of the day and night. Use the information just given to help you to identify the times at which the different phases of your daily cycle occur. Make notes in your logbook.

Specific Method

Another method of discovering our daily cycles is to notice the direction in which our energy is moving. With a little practice, everyone seems able to do this; that is, to discover whether their energy is moving in, out, or is in balance. The way to do this is simple and outlined in the following exercise.

Exercise 3: Observing the Flow and Direction of Life Energy.

Step 1: As you concentrate on grounding and centring, cultivate general awareness of your body. Gain an overall impression of the sensations you are having. Notice how physically energetic you seem, how vital, or how slowed down or reflective you are. As you do, also notice any sense you have of a direction in your energy. Ask yourself several questions:

1. Is my energy moving in or out?
2. Is my energy balanced?
3. On a scale of 0 to 10, how much flow do I have? (Use 0 for balanced and 10 for maximum in-flow or out-flow).
4. Am I moving towards or away from a peak?

Note your answers in your logbook.

Step 2: Answering four more questions can help if you are still uncertain about the flow and direction of your life energy. Ask yourself:

1. What would I do if I did precisely what my body wants right now?
2. Would I become more active? ('Yes' implies out-flow)
3. Would I become less active? ('Yes' implies in-flow)
4. Would I balance things more? ('Yes' implies a transition)

As usual, note your answers in your logbook.

THE CYCLES

You can see a pattern common to many people in the diagram earlier in the chapter. It has our energies starting in the transition between the outward phase and the inward phase. There is no flow in or out during this stage. The time of the first of these transitions in our day will vary from person to person.

Generally, the full daily pattern is completed after we have experienced both phases twice. The peaks of the outward phases, when our energies are moving out most strongly, and the peaks of the inward phases, when our energies are moving in most strongly, are shown in the figure where the wave line turns back towards the midline in the diagram. When on the midline, we are in transition. As we approach these peaks, our energy flow gradually increases; as we pass the peaks, our energy flow gradually reduces again, until it ceases during the next time of transition.

More specifically, as we enter the outward phase, we become progressively more aware of and attentive to the outside. In this phase, our energies have changed direction from in-flow to outflow, with the strength of out-flowing energy increasing. This draws us naturally into those activities, experiences and perceptions already outlined. The turning point occurs at the peak flow of the outward phase, after which the impulse to activity, initiative and engagement begins to diminish and keeps doing so until it reaches the transition between this phase and the inward phase that follows.

Entering the inward phase is similar, in that we have an increasingly intense experience of a natural receptivity and inclination to be inward-looking. This will reach a peak and then, as we begin to move away from this peak, we find ourselves becoming less intensely drawn to the inside and less strongly inclined to act in the ways that are consistent with this phase. After a while, we again move into transition.

As mentioned above, there is no single pattern for everyone, so avoid assuming this common pattern is true of you. For example, some people go through the full cycle more or less than twice every 24 hours, have several peaks in either the outward phase or the inward phase of the cycle, or the outward (or inward) phase may be more sustained than the inward (outward) one.

Exercise 4: Identifying Your Unique Daily Cycle. Monitor your cycle through several days. Note when you seem to have a lot of out-flowing energy and when the flow seems to go inwards. Also, notice tne intensity and direction, so you can develop a sense of the timing of the peaks of each phase. As you work out your patterns, draw them on the figure below.

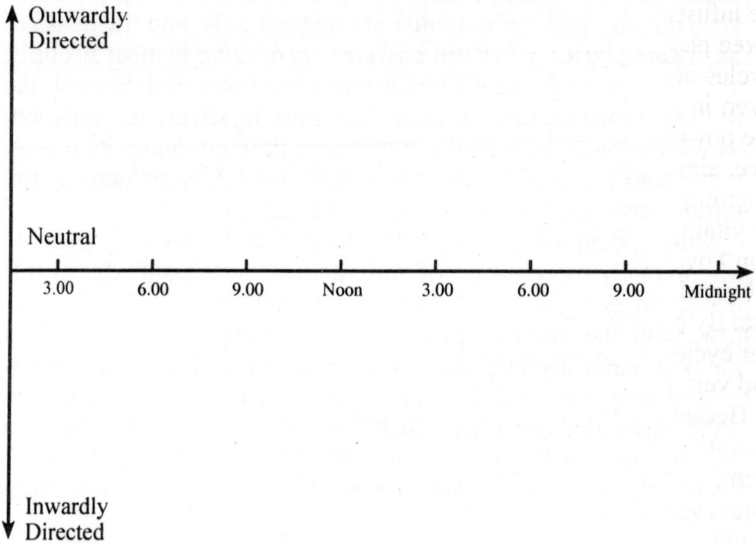

Mapping Your Daily Cycles

21
Living Cyclically

When we synchronise what we do with our daily cycles, we can be infused with wonderful vitality and abundant energy during all three phases – inward, outward and transition. Aligning with our cycles also promotes wellbeing and awakens inspiration. Moreover, in the world of today, this alignment can help us to manage the powerful pressures placed on us to keep working and stay active, almost no matter what else is going on in our lives. Through aligning ourselves we can lead busy lives and maintain a sense of vitality, balance and enjoyment – provided, of course, that we don't overdo it. This proviso is very important. We can even finish a busy day, week, month or year feeling fresh and interested in life. By contrast, when we live with our activities misaligned with our cycles, we tend to become hyped up, clogged up or drained – and very uncomfortable.

Because our natural energy cycles are like breathing, if we cooperate with them, our lives are much easier; if we ignore or fight them, our lives are much harder. For example, if we keep forcing ourselves to stay active when in an inward phase, then it is like trying to keep breathing out when we have run out of air in our lungs. Similarly, if we keep trying to keep still and reflective when we have moved into an outward phase, it is like trying to keep breathing in when our lungs are full of air. Both these responses significantly disrupt our sense of wellbeing, our capacity to function, the ease with which we live our lives and our availability to the Infinite. They also lead to congestion in our systems.

ALIGNING WITH OUR CYCLES

The following two simple principles help with this alignment. One relates to *what* we do, and the other to *the way* we do it.

Principle 1: Choose what to do so it aligns with the current phase in your daily cycle.

Principle 2: Adjust your style of doing things so it aligns with the current phase in your daily cycle.

Choosing What to Do and How to Do It

Some activities are more aligned or consistent with each phase than others. Being aware of this is very helpful because, with a little thought, we can make what we do consistent with each phase. Also, when planning ahead we can schedule our activities so they align with the phases we will enter later on.

Let's imagine that we are planning for the day and we know that we are in an outward phase from mid-morning to early afternoon, at which time we go through a transition followed by an inward phase. What can we do?

From mid-morning, we can organise to do the things requiring alertness, energy, activity, initiative and the handling of a lot of demands. For the transition phase, we can plan activities that call on our natural inclination to evaluate what we have been doing, to become aware of loose ends and to anticipate what is to come. For when the transition ends and the in-flow starts, we can organise to do slower more routine activities than the morning ones. The table below has specific examples of what we can do in each phase.

Inward Phase	Transition	Outward Phase
Move easily and slowly	Move with poise and balance	Move vigorously and quickly
Talk quietly, softly	Talk moderately, easily	Talk more loudly, strongly
Ask questions	Listen, pay active attention	Make statements
Relax	Do balanced activity	Exercise
Be receptive	Wait alertly and openly	Take the initiative
Allow others to make contact	Allow flexibility of approach	Make contacts actively
Ask for/invite help	Contemplate what is needed	Give or offer help
Ruminate, gestate	Cultivate alert awareness	Analyse, plan
Do easy routine things	Consider what is coming	Face challenges, deal with complexity
Be inactive	Allow reflective action	Be active
Use telephone, email, texting	Plan, schedule	Go visiting
Contemplate projects	Make notes on projects	Work on projects, act
Lie, sit, lean	Move around easily	Stand, walk, run

Some Activities Related to the Phases of Daily Cycles

Clearly, when making plans, using to-do lists and considering priorities will also be important (see Chapters 5 to 7).

Exercise 1: Matching Activities to Daily Cycles.

Step 1: Identify the current phase of your daily cycle right now. Think about what you are doing or are about to do. If necessary, modify *what you are doing* and *the way you are doing it* to suit the phase that is current for you. Note your activities and styles in your logbook.

Step 2: Now also think ahead to tomorrow. Using your usual daily cycle as a template, plan your activities as much as you can so they are aligned with the three different phases. Note this program in your logbook. Of course, once you become familiar with this process, you can create a general schedule by assigning your regular activities to certain times and days of the week. When you do, record your general schedule in your logbook, too.

Managing Out-of-Phase Times

These plans are all very well, but what about the many times we are not free to do what we want? The demands on us don't always occur at convenient times or in ways that align with our daily cycles. For example, we may be required to act vigorously when we are well into an inward phase; or the only opportunity to sleep may be when we are at the height of an outward phase. What to do is, in principle, very simple.

When in an inward phase, the idea is to do the same things that we usually do but more slowly and languidly. For example, pick up and dial the telephone more slowly, talk more quietly, walk more sedately. Engage people in a relaxed way. While doing these things, relax your body so its tension is released and your energy is conserved. Far from interfering in performance, these approaches usually increase efficiency and effectiveness.

> *Take for example the profession of teaching. When alert and vital, during the outward phase, it is easy to stand up, move around, talk with animation, actively engage students, and teach with vitality. When experiencing the inward phase, it is much less easy to do things this way, and it is often costly to try. What a teacher can do instead is, for example, sit down or lean against a wall when teaching instead of standing upright; ask questions of the students instead of presenting*

information; talk more quietly and more slowly, or give students assignments to do. Far from being less effective, as many people in performing jobs often anticipate they will be, this approach is more effective. Students (and others) learn more, and are more available when their teachers are well grounded and centred, because they don't have to deal with the teacher's energetic turbulence while learning what is being taught.

By contrast, if we have to slow down in an outward phase and do something reflective, restrained or introspective, the idea is to do what is required in the way it is required. Staying grounded and centred will help. However, in order to have an outlet for our abundant energy, we can identify things we can do that don't disrupt the primary activity. We may get up and move around slowly to do our thinking, take frequent breaks to do some exercise, or do mildly expressive things like offering to make notes (or take minutes) for everyone.

Think of someone trying to sleep while entering an outward phase. People often lie there wanting to slow down and go to sleep, but discover that their systems become more alert. What they can do is lie still, stay as grounded and relaxed as possible, and stop trying to go to sleep. Instead, they can simply accept the outflow and relax into or flow with it. Compared with sleeping unconsciously, this may give them a different sort of rest; however, when they get used to relaxing like this, they discover it is restful and refreshing.

Changing Style

Three practical steps can help us decide what to do when we have no freedom to change what we are doing and need to change style:

1. Stay grounded and centred (see Chapters 9 to 12).
2. Identify the current phase of our cycles (see Chapter 20).
3. Keep doing what is necessary by adjusting the style of doing it to align with the current phase.

Exercise 2: Adjusting Activity Styles When Out of Phase. During the next few days, notice the times when you need to act out of phase with your daily cycle. Adjust the way you do what you have to do so you continue doing it in a way that is aligned with your current phase. As soon as you can after the event, make notes of the results in your logbook.

ENERGY CHANGES DIRECTION, NOT INTENSITY

Our energy operates within a fairly well-defined range most of the time. Certainly we move from feeling tired and in need of rest, to feeling vital and full of energy. These fluctuations are natural. However, if we consider their intensity, the levels of this generally stay much the same. It is the quality of the energy, and direction and speed of its flow that varies. Our experience of the level of intensity, however, will usually vary very little.

22
A Conflict-Resolution Map

When were you last in conflict with someone? Do you have regular disagreements? How do you manage conflict? Do you have a particular style; for example, getting caught up in things, rigidly holding your position, or letting go of what is important to you? Or do you know how to approach others so you resolve things?

Whatever your answers are to these questions, when you are in conflict with others, it is often useful to have a map to help navigate your way to resolution. This is particularly so when situations are complex, when passions are high or when you are caught up in unhelpful processes.

In this chapter, we discuss general guidelines for managing conflicts, ways of encouraging everyone involved to continue working towards resolution, and techniques for managing conflict so our passions and feelings contribute towards resolution instead of disrupting it. The principles for setting goals and priorities are relevant here (see Chapters 5 to 7).

GUIDELINES FOR MANAGING CONFLICT

There are five main guidelines for managing conflict:

Guideline 1: Imagine and keep imagining a perfect outcome. This approach is clearly important when we remember our discussion of goal-setting (see Chapter 6). We need to start with where we want to finish. Remember, too, the value of keeping our attention on full resolution. If we do this, we are much more likely to end negotiations with everyone understanding the value of the outcome and with no one having compromised themselves to reach the resolution. This may sound all very well in theory, but what about in practice? Well, it certainly works better than starting off with the opposite expectations and approaches, as many ongoing personal and worldwide conflicts attest.

Guideline 2: Concentrate the discussion on what is already shared and build on this. When we follow this guideline, we can reach resolution more easily because knowing our common ground encourages cooperation, mutual respect, resolution and mutual understanding. Many seemingly impossible situations are resolved easily or more easily soon after the parties realise that they have interests, objectives, needs and other things in common. Also, what we share we intensify, so it is common sense to intensify the harmony we already share and build from there, instead of continuing to intensify our disputes.

Guideline 3: Seek real resolution and continue the process until it is reached. As part of this guideline, it is helpful to cultivate a preparedness to change our views, to shift positions, or to describe things differently – provided these changes are genuine. Genuine compromise can promote resolution and new understanding. By contrast, compromising ourselves by pretending agreement or understanding tends only to lead to later problems as unresolved issues and repressed energies re-surface.

Guideline 4: Safety is always of first importance. Some people in conflict resort to physical violence in order to bully others, to protect themselves from perceived threats, or out of desperation about what else to do. Whatever the reason, it is most important to reach agreements between all concerned that there will be no acts or threats of violence under any circumstance. If others are unwilling to guarantee their behaviour, we need to find ways of continuing negotiations so everyone is adequately protected. With interpersonal conflicts, one approach is to leave the scene as quickly as we can if violence erupts or is threatened. The same thing applies with verbal violence. While not physical, verbal abuse and harassment are deeply damaging to all involved. Remember, safety comes first.

Guideline 5: Celebrate every success. Encouragement is always helpful. When we acknowledge success, breakthroughs and resolutions as they occur, even if they are only small, they tend to multiply. Shared congratulations have a way of softening positions, leading to real flexibility, and promoting mutual respect and understanding. Also, we are rewarding each other for our efforts during the process, instead of waiting until the end.

Exercise 1: Managing a Simple Conflict. Think of a minor conflict you have with someone at present. Think about each of the five guidelines you have just read and apply them to your conflict. Go as far as you can with these alone. Make notes in your logbook about any changes you experience in your attitudes and expectations. Maybe show the others involved this part of the book and discuss the suggestions. Seek agreement with whoever else is involved on how to proceed.

MANAGING DIRECTION

Four simple steps that can help us to keep our efforts productive as we seek to resolve conflicts are:

1. Set goals clearly.
2. Discuss these goals with each other.
3. Take breaks when necessary.
4. Persist until resolution is reached.

Step 1: Set goals clearly. All parties can benefit from taking the time to consider what is important in relation to the people, situations and events involved. Making lists is a good idea. When our goals are clear, we can use them throughout the discussions/negotiations to keep evaluating whether our actions are likely to promote or interfere with resolution.

Step 2: Share and discuss those goals. We begin the discussions with everyone stating and explaining their goals, hopes, dreams, desires, and aspirations – in terms of what they want, of course! This is not a time for struggle, persuasion, or contention. It is best if each person has a turn without anyone interrupting. This provides an opportunity for everyone to discover what is important to each of the others and to identify common ground.

Step 3: Take breaks when necessary. Taking a break can make the difference between staying in an impasse and moving through it to resolution. During a break, we often understand things differently, sometimes because the pressure is off, sometimes because time-out gives us the chance to adjust our positions or to digest the learning we are doing about other people's priorities. (This last process is discussed in more detail later.)

To illustrate, think of a fly or a bee that mindlessly continues to try to fly through a windowpane. Some do this until they die, clearly not realising that their efforts are futile. When we are acting similarly, by mindlessly and repetitively doing things that don't work, taking a break can help us 'move back from the glass', notice that there is an opening nearby and fly through it to freedom.

Step 4: Persist until resolution is reached. Persistence and patience are often important. With persistence – for hours, days, months, or years, if necessary – most situations are resolvable. We need to appreciate that people can change and that resolving conflicts often requires us to make real personal change ourselves, particularly if intense feelings are involved. Persistence gives us all the opportunity to take care of our own intensity and the time to do our necessary learning and adjusting.

Exercise 2: Staying on Track for Resolution. Consider the conflict from the last exercise, or another mild one; then engage with the other person involved. Discuss the five guidelines and four steps and seek agreement to use them to resolve the issues. Again, make notes in your logbook about the results you get. You can do it!

MANAGING INTENSITY

During conflict, it is often the intensity of feeling that creates the major challenge, particularly when we allow these feelings to overpower rationality, common sense and good intentions. This impedes progress towards worthwhile resolution, so having some means of dealing with intensity is a great asset. What follows is offered as just one way of taking care of this aspect of conflict. There are five steps to the process:

1. Engage in discussions.
2. Stop when the discussions become non-productive; and maybe go off alone.
3. Concentrate on personal resolution during this pause.
4. Return to the discussions.
5. Repeat steps 1 to 4 until the issues are resolved.

Step 1: Engage in discussions. Resolution can be reached with most people under most circumstances, provided we stay engaged with each other. If people will not talk or communicate in some way, then very little is likely to change.

Step 2: Stop when the discussions become non-productive. When discussing contentious issues or difficulties, it is both easy and common to become embroiled in non-productive, cyclic processes that everyone involved knows will lead nowhere.

This is the time to take a break, because resolution has become less important to us than acting out our parts of the conflict. Continuing to try to negotiate will generally feed the conflict, while stopping offers us a good chance to release ourselves from our parts in it.

A good idea is to agree in advance about stopping at times like this. To make this stopping easy, it often helps to consider how to interrupt when our disruptive emotional patterns are interfering.

Some people use particular words ('Oops, we're doing it again'), gestures (a warding-off gesture of the hand, a touch on an arm), or doing something humorous (putting on a silly hat). Each of us needs to come up with a signal that works for us, tell the others involved, agree to stop when these signals are used with us, and take a break. Just before breaking, it also helps to make a commitment about when everyone will return.

Step 3: Concentrate on personal resolution. These breaks are designed to promote resolution, not block it. They give us time to deal with the personal issues that are contributing to our parts in the conflict, and the time to resolve what is stirring in us. These are generally to do with unfinished business from our pasts. We need to use what works to calm ourselves and start thinking clearly at these times. The following three suggestions may help with this.

(a) Do something different, preferably something enjoyable. We can do this alone or with the others involved in the conflict. When we do it with the others, we don't mention or discuss our difficulties. This is a time for shifting our attention. The fun and enjoyment often make release much easier than if we do something serious. Having an enjoyable meal, watching a funny movie, playing music we like, or spending time with carefree people are all good options.

(b) Do the Grounding Meditation. This is a very powerful method for resolving past difficulties, dealing with passions in the present and clarifying our thinking about the future (see Chapters 9 and 10). We can use the recording to give ourselves external support. Repeating the meditation as many times as it takes for us to reach complete equilibrium, or at least enough balance to get back into productive discussions, is important. To test our readiness, we can think about our discussions and notice if we react in the same way as we did before we took the break. If we do, we have more grounding to do. We go back into the discussions when we are in equilibrium again, provided the others are also ready. The equilibrium is not necessarily a state of calmness, although it is helpful if we have reached that.

(c) Do the Unifying Meditation. This meditation is introduced in the next chapter. We can use a recording for this[38], particularly if we need external support to stay on track. This meditation is designed to help us deal with our personal involvement in any sort of conflict. Practising it regularly also helps to strengthen our commitments and capacities to live cooperatively.

As in (b), we know we are ready to return to the discussions when we experience a sufficient sense of personal equilibrium, resolution and release.

Step 4: Return to the discussions. This is most important. The whole point of the break is to take time so we resolve our own part in the conflict. We take a break to promote resolution, not to avoid it. When we return to our discussions after such a break, we usually think, feel and act more freely and openly about the previously contentious issues.

Step 5: Keep repeating the first four steps until resolution is reached. After returning to the discussions, we may quickly move towards a resolution that suits everyone. However, particularly when we are engaged in conflicts that are intense or long-standing, we may again get caught up in non-productive exchanges. If so, the best approach is to repeat the above steps: stop, take time out for grounding and personal resolution, return to the discussion. Stopping repeatedly, as above, usually helps us to deal with the multi-layered issues that are often present in conflicts. The overall result is that we all become progressively clearer and freer, and develop increasing confidence that resolution is possible. Once we experience this, full accord is often imminent.

It is worth repeating that persistence and patience are fundamental in this process. And they bring rewards. Even when it may seem as if the whole process is a waste of time, or too intense and difficult, it is worth persisting. Every step produces further progress towards resolution – every step – even when we don't seem to be making progress. With some conflicts, it may even take years. Nevertheless, when resolution comes, our patience is wonderfully rewarded.

Exercise 3: Dealing with Intense Feelings. Consider a current conflict, and, using the five steps just outlined, do your best to resolve it. Rather than trying to learn everything at once, however, using one guideline or taking one step at a time (practising them) is often the best way to learn what to do. Log your results in your book.

23
Releasing Ourselves from Conflict

Harmony, oneness, cooperation and mutual respect are natural to human beings, although we can easily get the opposite impression a lot of the time. I-Am, which is the essence of our worldly selves, is saturated in these qualities, and meditation and other practices can help us to release ourselves into their constancy (see Chapters 1, 2, 11 and 13). Note this: I-Am is the power that prompts us and perpetually draws us towards resolution. Even so, most of us face conflicts from time to time and can benefit from having specific practices that help to release us effectively from them.

THREE PRINCIPLES

Some conflicts are internal (e.g., between wanting to do something and knowing it is bad for us); some are between ourselves and others (e.g., between us and our mothers or fathers, us and work colleagues); and some are between other people (e.g., between two friends, two strangers). The following three principles can help us to understand what we are dealing with in any conflict and help us to manage our parts in what is occurring.

Principle 1: Our perceptions of the world around us and what is done to us are replicas of our inner processes.
Put another way: the outside is a replica of our insides. Everything we observe in the people, situations and events around us is also true of us and has been stimulated by those aspects in us. For example, if I think someone is angry, then I have similar anger in me; if I feel someone is loving, then I have similar love in me; if I perceive two people arguing over something, then the same sort of argument is in me; and if I observe others who are loving, secure, vital, healthy, or adequate, then those experiences and qualities are available in me as well. This is a wonderfully empowering thing to understand about ourselves. All the same, it can take time for us to accept that this is always true no matter what the circumstances.

Principle 2: Oneness within and oneness with others is our natural state.
This means that everything is fundamentally integrated, aligned, cooperative, respectful, clear and harmonious, which explains, at least in part, why it takes tremendous energy to keep ourselves in contracted or divided states. In other words, it takes much more energy and effort to stay in conflict within or with others than to be in harmony. This may also challenge some long-held views.

Principle 3: Staying aware of our responses and staying grounded and centred restores our fundamental oneness more easily.
This last principle means that conflict can only be maintained within if we allow ourselves to become ungrounded or uncentred. When we encourage our systems to stay grounded and centred, no matter how stimulating and challenging this may be at times, our systems cannot easily contract, split, harden up or store enmity.

UNIFYING MEDITATION

The *Unifying Meditation* is a simple method of releasing our part in any conflict. As already noted, whenever we experience or observe conflict, our inner version of it simultaneously becomes active. The *Unifying Meditation* can release us from conflict by freeing us from our own conflicts and our tendencies towards perceiving lack of accord in ourselves or others. It also helps us to actively promote unity, cooperation, clarity and mutual respect.[39]

This meditation produces deep and lasting change within us. The resultant freedom from conflicts is truly wonderful. Amazingly, and quite frequently, others whom we include in the meditation also change quite dramatically and are much less likely to involve us in conflict from then on.

Using all three of the above principles to secure our release, the meditation gets us to claim a state of oneness at the beginning of the resolution process. It helps us to use whatever the conflict is as a way of accessing our inner replica of that conflict. It then enables us to relive this so we can release ourselves from it.

THE MEDITATION

There are four main steps and each has a number of parts to it.

1. Getting started:
    - Consider what you want to change.

- Select a conflict (people, groups, organisations, etc that are polarised).
- Imagine everything is perfect.

2. Resolve, harmonise, digest or release the conflict:
   - Imagine you are the first person or part of the conflict (Polarity #1 in the diagram).
   - Imagine you are the second person or other part of the conflict (Polarity #2 in the diagram).
   - Imagine you are the exchanges between these two people or parts (Conflicting Interactions in the diagram).
3. Perfect the relationship:
   - Imagine perfection within, around and between the two people or parts.
   - Imagine you are one with this perfection.
4. Live the oneness:
   - Choose something to do that is consistent with the imagined perfection.
   - Do this as soon as possible.

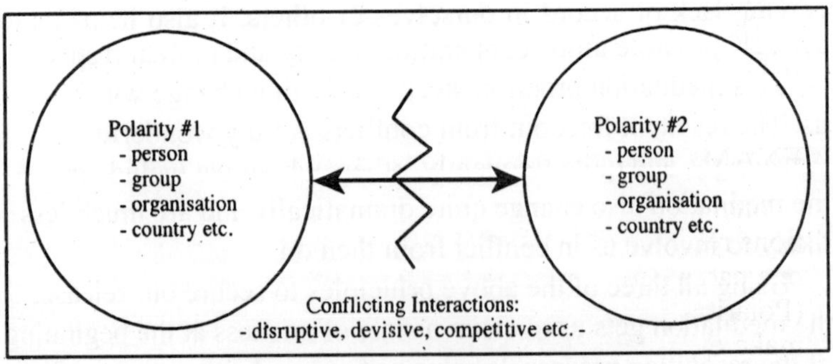

Conflicts Involve Two Polarised Positions
and Interactions that Maintain the Polarities

The meditation works by helping unify both all parts of us that are polarised and our conflictual interactions. In the process, we claim through identification and physical acting out (safely, privately and alone) each side of a conflict (each polarity). We attempt to live each one by moving around and adopting related postures, gestures, voice tones, etc. We may experience reluctance to do this, but experiencing each side as fully as we can is fundamental to our resolution. Then we claim the conflicting interactions by embracing both sides of the conflict and opening ourselves fully to the internal aspects of the exchanges. The final step – doing something that is consistent with the resolution we have been imagining – helps to realign us with our ideal outcome.

It is important that we concentrate on grounding throughout, as it is fundamental to the success of the meditation. Aside from helping us to deal with the great energy that we may release as we proceed, the grounding helps to promote integration, harmony, transparency, sweetness and fragrance in ways that heal, soothe and release us. Centring is another key to final success (see Chapters 9 to 12) because it helps to flood us with life energy throughout the process. Both meditations help to release us from the whole conflict by digesting its separate elements.

Sometimes we reach full resolution after one meditation, while at other times more than one is necessary, particularly for long-standing and intense issues. If you find that many repetitions are necessary, take heart, because after every one there is less to do than there was before. In my experience, those who persist, even in the face of intense discomfort, have always been rewarded, often in ways that were beyond their most cherished dreams.

The following example of a man who is in conflict with his wife over the family budget illustrates the steps of the meditation in a domestic setting. (Use the diagram throughout to guide you.)

EXAMPLE

Step 1: Getting started. The man considers the various situations related to his concerns about money. He selects his wife as one part of the conflict (Polarity #1) and himself as the other part (Polarity #2). He then imagines for several minutes what would make everything perfect. He needs to remember to do this fully, without holding back just because he is upset with his wife at the time. Then he concentrates on grounding and centring again.

Step 2: Resolve the inner conflict. With this second step, the man begins with his wife (Polarity #1) and imagines for several minutes that he is her in the middle of the conflict with him: he imagines that he looks like her, sounds like her, thinks like her, feels like her, moves like her, smells like her, and says what she says – he is her in every imaginable way. And in private he acts out all of this (as above). Pretending he is an actor, he becomes one with her part in the conflict as he perceives it. Then for several minutes he concentrates on grounding and centring again.

The next move is for him to claim himself, the other part of the conflict (Polarity #2), and to imagine himself in the midst of the conflict with his wife. For several minutes he imagines and acts out how he looks, sounds, thinks, feels, moves, smells, acts and what he says when they are in the midst of their conflict. He does his best to become one with his part in the conflict. Then he concentrates on grounding and centring again for several minutes.

After this, he turns his attention, also for several minutes, to what takes place between he and his wife during the conflict (Conflicting Interactions). He does this by imagining that both he and his wife have combined inside him, that he is both of them together, and that he is aware of and acts out what is happening between them. What is happening may be something obvious, such as words, gestures, or physical acts; it may be subtle, such as covert looks, little changes of posture or voice tone; or there may be no apparent exchange. Whatever he notices, he makes himself one with it. He then concentrates on grounding and centring again.

Step 3: Perfecting the relationship. With the third step, the man takes his time to imagine that both he and his wife are perfectly happy with each other: that everything has worked out perfectly for them both. He imagines this specifically, or generally, depending on what he is considering, and he again acts out what he is imagining. Then he identifies himself with this perfection as fully as he can in order to embrace it completely and become one with every aspect of the perfection that he is imagining. Then he concentrates on grounding and centring again.

Step 4: Living the oneness. The last step involves overt action. The man thinks of the kinds of things he would do routinely, if everything were fine with his wife and they were in harmony; he selects one that he will do as an expression of his imagined resolution; then he does whatever it is as soon as possible. Of course, as he makes his choice, it is important for him to consider the likely consequences of his action and to choose realistically.

The point of this last step is to enact our internal unification and resolution in the external world. This anchors or fixes the changes we have made during the meditation in our daily lives. Up to this point, the whole process has been internal and we need to externalise it. Even insignificant acts are enough for this purpose and can make a difference. As a way of expressing his resolution, he might, for example, buy her flowers, or do something at home that she would like. Interestingly, the other people involved (e.g., the wife) don't need to know what is behind these acts for them to serve their purpose as part of the unifying.

Meditation 1: Unifying a Simple Conflict. Choose a mild conflict you currently have with someone. (It is often easier to start with a small challenge.) Then, using the written instructions above or the recording, do the *Unifying Meditation*. At the end, use your logbook to document your reactions and what has changed for you. Keep repeating the meditation at least once a day for several days, and stay alert for improvements between you and the other person.

24
Effective Decision-Making

We make decisions every moment of our lives: when to stand, what to do, how to move, what to say, where to look, when to leave home, when to go to work, how to say what we want, when to cook a meal, what to buy at the shops, how much money to spend, what to eat and when to eat it. With thousands of decisions an hour, it is obvious most are not made consciously. Many of them have become so routine that we are oblivious that we are making them. Nevertheless, whether we notice or not, we are perpetually making decisions: big, small and in-between.

Clearly, it is helpful to ensure that our decisions are good for us and others and will advance our happiness and fulfilment. However, many people don't understand decision-making, so in this chapter we briefly consider what decisions are, then discuss three different approaches to them: making decisions, evolving decisions and using the 10-10-10 system.

Exercise 1: Simple Decisions. For the next few days, note in your logbook ten simple decisions that you make each day. Note anything from tea-or-coffee type decisions to buying-or-not-buying-a-car type decisions. They are all relevant.

WHAT DECISIONS ARE

Definition: A decision is the internal 'act' that precedes or accompanies our overt behaviour.

Decisions always exist in relation to something – thoughts, feelings, impulses, behaviour, resources, directions, goals and many other things. Very importantly, they also involve choices between options.

Exercise 2: The Internal and External Aspects of Decisions: Consider what goes on inside you when you decide to do something like eating a meal, hurrying down the street, thinking about your budget, lying in bed, or feeling upset without doing anything to change your feelings. Now, also think about what is involved when you decide to change something by, for example, stopping eating, beginning to walk slowly down the street, thinking about the party tonight instead of budgeting, getting out of bed, or doing something enjoyable to change your current feelings. Make notes in your logbook.

Importantly, it is our actions that show what we have decided and not what we say or think we have decided. For example, no matter what people claim they have decided, a person who stays in bed has decided to do that instead of getting up; and a person who keeps eating has decided to keep eating even if vigorously claiming otherwise.

Principle 1: The action we take is the decision we made.
Genuine decisions expressed in words usually take the form, 'I did such and such', 'I'm doing such and such' and 'I will do such and such'. Statements like the following are 'pretend' decisions because they indicate a lack of commitment: 'I'll try to do …', 'I want to do…', 'I hope to do…', 'I wish I could do...' and 'I'll see if I can do…'[40] They almost always lead to inaction.

Exercise 3: Genuine and 'Pretend' Decisions. For the next week, notice the decisions you make. Record in your logbook at least two genuine decisions you made each day – genuine as indicated by the action you actually took; and two examples a day of 'pretend decisions', things that you did not follow through on.

Priorities and commitment are also involved in decision-making. We usually follow through more on our higher priorities than on our lower ones (see Chapter 7). We also usually commit more time and resources to achieving our higher priorities than our lower ones. This translates into a simple definition of commitments.

Definition: A commitment is a decision to devote time and resources to achieving a goal.

All the same, remember that any decision can be changed, although the consequences of changing some decisions may not stop the flow-on effects already started by earlier action. Even in the midst of something, however, we can decide to withhold further action and change what we are doing. For example, we can decide to stop talking for long enough to change our voice tone and what we are saying, or to convert a threatening act into a greeting.

MAKING DECISIONS

Definition: To *make a decision* we assess our options and choose between them.

We make many straightforward choices each day. 'Will I do this or that?' is the pattern of these choices. When we make them consciously, we generally take into account our goals, the so-called costs and benefits of each option, and any other consequences that might flow from our choices.

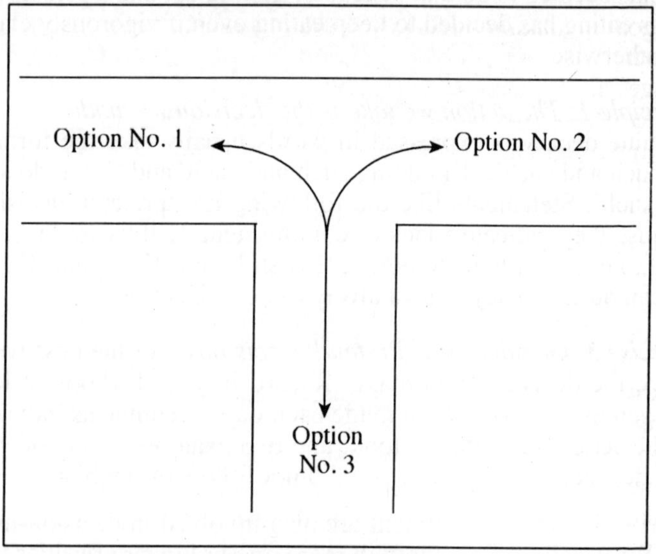

Making Decisions

In its simplest form, this process is like driving up to a T-intersection and deciding where to go next, as shown in this diagram. We have three main options: we can go right, or left, or return the way we came.

Let's say our goal is to have completed the shopping and to be home again within an hour. We know that the shopping itself will take about 30 minutes. We also know that going left to one set of shops will take 10 minutes, while going right to another set will take 20 minutes. This makes our choice obvious: we don't have enough time to go right and so we turn left. Under some circumstances, we might decide to return the way we came. For example, we may head back home immediately if we are held up in traffic before getting to the intersection and we arrive there too late to reach either set of shops.

Not all choices are clear-cut like this. In some complicated situations we may have many options to consider, we may not know the consequences of some of them and we may need time to investigate. Most of us are familiar with this process. The exercise that follows is one way of handling choices involving multiple options and complex consequences.

Exercise 4: Making Complex Decisions. Think about a decision you have wanted to make for some time. In your logbook, write your goal in making the decision then list the obvious options for achieving the goal. Under each option, write down two lists: advantages and disadvantages, and put a number from 1 to 10 beside each to indicate its significance or priority to you. (1 is for the least important and 10 for the most important.) When you have finished, add up the columns. The highest score wins: if 'yes' then maybe choose it; if 'no' then maybe not. At the end, notice if you are clearer on what your decision will be and record your reactions in your logbook.

EVOLVING DECISIONS

Think of a situation such as going into a new business venture, leaving a marriage, living in another country, choosing a profession, or deciding on the best school for your children. These and many other situations in life are not simple enough for us to make our decisions in the manner just described; their complexity involves too many different issues, people, events and situations. Also, the necessary information may be inaccessible and the consequences of the various possibilities unknown to us. Likewise, the results of previous action may still be unfolding or the current situation may be too changeable for us to know what to do.

Despite such complexity, however, many people still often try to *make these decisions* in the same way they decide what to put on their shopping lists. However, relying solely on the cost-benefit analysis approach rarely works out well in such situations. Most of us realise this, but don't know another way to deal with what we are facing. What we can do is *evolve our decisions* instead of trying to make them.

Definition: We *evolve a decision* when we give expression to or act out our various thoughts, perceptions, reactions or impulses as they arise, and keep doing this until we experience a sense of certainty or knowing about the best thing to do.

Acting out our reactions is central to this process. It involves doing something that physically moves our inner responses out into the world around us. By doing this, we express what is going on inside us and ground it. But, you may wonder, what if I want to do something really drastic? The answer is: we don't have to do that. We can choose to do something insignificant, which avoids risking anything. A little is a lot in this process. As long as we do something that directly expresses what is current for us, this is enough to support the evolution of the decision we are considering. For example, we start to think about selling our home. To do this as our first step could create significant complications, so instead, we look for the names of companies that sell houses.

Staying grounded and centred throughout the process is very important. Doing this helps us to keep digesting what we experience and to keep returning to a state of enlivened balance. Also, the idea is to regard every one of our responses as temporary, because the moment we express what is current for us, some other idea or impulse may arise that takes us in a completely different direction. This is an important part of the process and can lead to a lot of meandering around at times. However, this meandering is the way we discover and integrate all the different layers of our responses into our final decision.

The process is very simple. Take the example of deciding whether or not to go into a business partnership. On day one we feel enthusiastic, so we telephone our prospective partner to discuss various aspects of the potential partnership. On day two we begin to worry about, say, our prospective partner's reliability, so we contact others who know him and discuss how reliable he is in business.

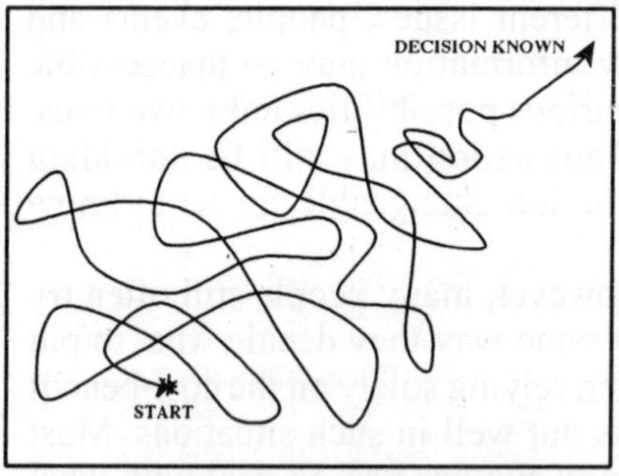

Evolving Decisions through Expressing Each Reaction as it Arises

Later that day, somewhat satisfied with the morning's contacts, we nevertheless still feel doubtful, so we put some files related to the deal that we had intended to read at home back in our desk drawer. Letting things rest for a while expresses our doubts. The next morning, we wake up feeling more certain about the advantages again, so we decide to deal with the files that day while at work. Then later that same day, some financial consequences of the deal occur to us, so we contact our bank manager or financial adviser to discuss them. And so the process continues. Eventually, we get to a definite point of resolution. And then we act.

A more domestic example would be a decision to terminate an established friendship. On day one we want to keep it, so we telephone our friend to say 'hello'. On day two we are doubtful again, so we find something we have borrowed in preparation for returning it when we say goodbye. We then have several wonderful memories of our friendship and decide to telephone our friend that night to talk about them. And so this process continues.

Notice how going through these steps enables us to express and experience many different layers of feelings, nuances of responses, common sense, contradictory impulses and desires, perceptiveness, illogical conclusions – anything and everything that is there. As we express what arises in us, our systems are clearing our histories and allowing us to become aware of what is deeply right for us, a knowing that may have been initially buried under many layers of accumulated living. Also, notice how what we choose to do at each point can be completely private, so we don't risk everything with each move. Even so, at times, in order to evolve into what we need to do, some very obvious steps might be necessary. Always remember to stay grounded and centred through each step.

The Point of Resolution is Obvious

After having experienced resolution once, you will always know when you reach it again in relation to other issues. When we have expressed the many different aspects involved for us in the decision we are evolving, we become completely clear and certain what to do. We simply know it. Our course of action has become obvious because we feel, think and perceive that it is right; we see the sense of it; and everything we hear and say adds up, too.

By contrast, any feelings or impulses to the contrary – any tension, anything we notice that implies that we are pretending, any hoping or craving for the end of the process, any hurrying or ways of not allowing our evolving understanding to complete itself – are indications that we have not yet reached the point of resolution.

Remember, just because we really want something to be 'right' for us, doesn't make it 'right'. We will know when it is, however, and need to keep evolving until we have that knowing.

Interestingly, even at the end of the process, the road ahead is not always smooth. Some decisions, while right for us, may involve hardship, distress or disruption for others or ourselves. However, when we have truly completed the evolving process, our conviction helps us to persist in what we need to do. It acts as a backstop and support. If this sense is absent, then we have another indication that we have more evolving to do before we are finished.

Experience has shown that, provided we complete the process, those of us who evolve our decisions like this find that it works well. What is often not obvious is how long the process will take, for it often starts without the end in sight.

Exercise 5: Evolving Decisions. Select at least one area of your life in which you have been undecided for some time. Think about the issues and your current responses. Then begin the process of evolving your decision. Keep notes in your logbook and keep evolving – that is, expressing your current responses – until you know with certainty what to do. Note the nature of this certainty in your logbook too.

10-10-10 DECISIONS

10-10-10 is a process conceived and developed by Suzy Welch[41], which helps us to manage the complexities involved in assessing the consequences of many of our choices. A wonderful adjunct to making and evolving decisions, its power is in its simplicity.

When faced with a decision, Suzy suggests that we ask ourselves a question and that we consider what the consequences of our various answers would be in 10 minutes (in the immediate future), 10 months (in the medium-term future) and 10 years (in the long-term future).[42] As we make these assessments, our priorities, our preferences, the practical consequences of our choices and many other dimensions may need to be considered. (In relation to our personal wellbeing, much of the material included in this book about priorities and about the health and other benefits that arise from the practices suggested could be directly relevant.)

Let's consider the following question using 10-10-10: *I'm too busy to practise what's in this book; should I do it anyway?*

Had I not already discovered the benefits, the following would be my answers as I faced the prospect of exploring and discovering the value of the information in this book.

What if I decide not to do the learning?

10 minutes: I will relieve myself of the immediate discomfort and pressure about doing something new. My life will continue as before.

10 months: I'll still be living as I am and possibly be in worse shape, as I'm already not taking care of myself as well as I should. I won't know what benefits I could have got from changing how I live. Many of the benefits are supposed to show long before 10 months, so if I'd started back then, I would already know if they were worth a try. In other words, I'll have let a worthwhile opportunity pass me by. I'll be wondering, 'Will this be my pattern for the rest of my life?' I'll have nagging doubts that it will be.

10 years: Unless a miracle happens, or I have some major life crisis that finally gets my attention, I'll be well down the track of self-neglect and ill health. I would have missed a prime opportunity. I'll be aware that I could have started something 10 years earlier that could have revolutionised my life and I would have had 10 years of benefit from doing it. If the claims are true about the difference these practices make to people in just nine months, just imagine the effects of having done them for 10 years, or imagine having done them for 20, 30 or more years!

What if I decide to do the learning?

10 minutes: I might be uncomfortable for a few minutes, but I can deal with that and the benefits promised far outweigh these temporary costs. Besides, I could reward myself with something pleasant after I do each practice. Also, as I master each one, I could have a special celebration.

10 months: If the predictions are correct, I'll have made a good beginning on many of the practices by then and I'll know if they are making a difference. If they aren't helpful by then, I would've only diverted myself for 10 months, and what is 10 months compared to a lifetime?

10 years: By this stage, if the predictions are correct, I'll know very clearly and my life will be transformed. If they aren't correct, I'll have discovered this long before and will have stopped. Also, if they are correct, I'll have 10 years of momentum behind what

I do each day to assure my personal wellbeing, my awakening and my oneness in the Infinite.

Years ago my answer was: 'I'll start learning these practices today. By doing this, I'll confirm or otherwise their value to me. Also, in order not to overload myself by trying to do too much too quickly, I'll learn them one at a time, using the exercises and meditations provided, and I'll keep learning them one at a time until I master them all. I'm not going to let immediate temporary discomfort or my current ignorance stop me from getting the benefits offered.'

Exercise 6: 10-10-10. Think of a problem you need to solve, a question you want to answer, or anything unfinished. Formulate a question and use 10-10-10 to find your answer. As you do this, you may discover that some aspects of your assessments are best made through evolving your understanding. Of course, eventually you will need to make your decision and demonstrate that you have by acting on it.

SECTION FOUR

ENLIVENING MEDITATIONS

25
MEDITATING FOR SPIRITUAL FULFILMENT

I was 13 when I had my first spiritual taste of something that I now know as I-Am and the Infinite. I felt alone and isolated at the time. My parents were overseas for 12 months; two of my brothers, one my twin, were living hundreds of kilometres away; and my oldest brother and I were living in our family home under the watchful eye of Mrs Fish, a stranger who was a trained mother craft nurse.

In my distress and loneliness, I prayed for a sign that the divine was looking after me. Unexpectedly and wonderfully, within moments I was filled with a sense of peace, fulfilment and healing that was complete in itself. I knew I needed nothing more in that moment than whatever this was. I also knew instantly that there was much more to life than I had previously understood. Regrettably, the experience, which I wanted to go on forever, only lasted a few moments. However, it prompted me to find ways of living so I could enter it at will, or better still, experience it all the time. My learning continues.

Millions of people seek this kind of fulfilment every day and experience themselves as incomplete until they are awakened enough to know its fullness. In fact, no matter how ineffective our efforts are at times, everything we do in our daily lives can be understood as our best attempts to realise completion, because, as I understand it, the Infinite is perpetually prompting us to align ourselves with it and guiding our every step until we do. This explains the deeply compelling yearning, the hollowness looking to be filled, the 'soul itch' that must be scratched that many people know – a yearning, hollowness or itch which is the Infinite prompting us to release ourselves from our confinement in space and time through oneness with I-Am.

There is a paradox here, of course. On one hand, we are already complete and the fulfilment that arises from experiencing or knowing this directly – from awakening to it – is already who we are fundamentally. On the other hand, everyday events can easily keep us caught in and contracted by our daily lives in ways that obscure the Infinite from our awareness. This can easily give us the impression that we have to work to become what we already are.

Fortunately, to resolve this paradox, we don't need to re-engineer ourselves. All that is needed is for us to embrace the experience and knowing of each moment. Fulfilment does not come through trying to shed our naturalness, through denying our moment by moment awareness, through seeking to be someone or something we are not, or through adopting ways of acting that split us from who we are in the world. We are living, breathing bodily beings with worldly needs, wants, survival necessities and wondrous creative capacities. Celebrating and living all of this is the best means of becoming fulfilled in the Infinite.

Meditation offers many ways to celebrate and live what we already are and thus to find this fulfilment. But to benefit from it, we need to give meditation a significant place in our lives, rather than keeping it on the edges. In fact, meditation, family, work, leisure and friends all need to become central to us. This may require some reorganisation. However, it is worth it.

The meditations in the following chapters offer a variety of powerful, straightforward ways of learning basic inner skills and orientations. These can help us in our everyday lives and can be of particular help in opening us to oneness with the Infinite.

DIFFERENT ORIENTATION

To this point in the book, we have mainly concentrated on meditation as an accompaniment of everyday life. There have been some exceptions; however, our primary orientation was to introduce and master ways of living so the various practices became well integrated into what we normally do.

In the next five chapters, we will concentrate on meditations that promote spiritual awakening and fulfilment. They can also be integrated into our daily lives; however the most benefit from them arises when we set time aside, even if only brief periods, specifically to meditate in the ways outlined. The concentrated attention this makes possible is significant. Of course, beginning to do this may offer challenges, but Chapters 31 to 33 contain suggestions on how to introduce meditation and other new practices into our lives so the process is as easy as possible.

26
BREATHING MEDITATIONS

Breathing meditations energise our systems, clear our consciousness, distil unfinished business, expand our awareness and open us to I-Am and the Infinite. They bring rapid results and are worthwhile additions to our meditative repertoires. They also combine beautifully with the other practices in this book.

The use of breathing meditations has a long history. For example, they are central in some Taoist, Zen, Buddhist, Tantric and Pranayama Yoga practices.[43] In the West, breathing meditations also accompany the practice of *mindfulness meditation* that has become popular there in the last two decades.[44]

BENEFITS

Breathing meditations have powerful effects on our bodies, our feelings, our thinking and our awakening. They often help with grounding and energising. In principle, they are very simple as well: ongoing awareness of the breath is the primary orientation in virtually all of them.

In some of these meditations, we simply observe the breath; in others we observe and manage our breathing; and, in still others, we also meditate on certain images, fantasies or inner processes.

These meditations help us to:

- Improve concentration and attention span
- Learn acceptance of our experience
- Encourage emotional and mental wellbeing
- Keep us physically aware
- Keep us in the 'I-Am here-and-now'
- Charge our bodies with life energy
- Control and channel our life energy
- Distil our bodily, feeling, thinking, and spiritual energies
- Enter serene and transcendent states
- Promote alertness

SIMPLE BREATHING MEDITATION

The meditation that follows, like many others, has dual qualities: it gets us started and is so fundamentally powerful that it automatically takes us into many different levels of advanced practice as we master it. It is worth making it a part of your life.

Meditation 1: Basic Breathing Meditation.

Step 1: Sit or stand upright in a comfortable position. Begin your meditation by becoming grounded and centred.

Step 2: When ready, pay attention to your breathing. Remain relaxed and accept whatever you notice. You are not trying to do anything with your breathing, simply to notice it. You can notice the air moving into and out of your body, its sound, the way it feels, the changes of muscle tension, the rise and fall of your chest, the flow of air in and out of your nostrils. Notice any aspect of your breathing that enables you to keep track of it.

Step 3: From time to time, if you find that you have stopped noticing your breathing or are distracted by your thinking, gently guide your awareness back to your breathing. You can try the naming process, too, if that helps: 'breathing in', 'breathing out', 'pausing', 'heavy breath', 'slow breathing', 'distracted', etc.

Step 4: Occasionally, repeat the grounding and centring. When you finish, make notes in your logbook.

As we become accustomed to this meditation, we can do it regularly in many different situations. We can also combine with others; for example, with *The Awakening Meditation* (see Chapters 13 and 30), the *Inner Smile* and *Body Clenching Meditations* (see Chapter 27), and the *Relaxation Meditation* (see Chapter 16).

At times, we can become so clear when meditating like this that our breathing suspends fully, or the transitions at the end of the in-breath or out-breath become extended. At these times we become flooded with the type of experience I recounted in the last chapter. The *Relaxation Meditation* can also help to produce this.

27
Inner Smile & Body Clenching

We move now to another ancient meditation. Taoist in origin, it is called the *Inner Smile Meditation.*[45] Many people are surprised that so much can come from an act as simple as smiling. Yet, smiling releases our inner healer and comforter. Alone, the meditation can contribute a great deal to our health, general wellbeing and our spiritual fulfilment. When done with other meditations, it greatly enriches the effects they produce.

The *Inner Smile Meditation* helps with inner maintenance, with healing and with our alignment in the I-Am-here-and-now. It encourages increased flow of life energy through our personal systems. Using the meditation we can greatly accelerate our success with any goal. It also helps us to feel happy.

SMILING

You probably don't need a description of what smiling is; however, it's here just in case you do! The act of smiling involves crinkling the eyes at the corners and lifting the corners of the mouth. Try it now. Even just saying or reading the word 'smile' can start us doing it. But if you don't want to enjoy yourself, watch out! Smiling is definitely infectious and might take over without you meaning it to.

Smiles work very quickly, sometimes instantly. Folklore tells us that it takes far fewer muscles to smile than to frown, suggesting that it is easier to smile our way through life than not. We seem conditioned to smile, too. We notice when someone smiles at us and we generally experience an urge to smile back. Even little babies smile in response to our smiles.

Interestingly, the effects of smiling are physical, not just psychological and social. The physical act of smiling releases neurotransmitters in our brains: serotonin and endorphin. These chemicals influence our moods. Serotonin directly stimulates happiness at the same time as it reduces our sensitivity to pain; while endorphin provides direct pain relief.

WHAT AN 'INNER SMILE' IS

During the Inner Smile Meditation we direct our smiling energy towards the whole or individual parts of our bodies. The process is very much the same as smiling at people and them smiling back. Inside our bodies, our cells act and react similarly to people. When we smile at them, they respond with pleasure and 'smile' back. This may seem fanciful; however, it isn't.

Body Cells and Consciousness

Perhaps the most significant thing to understand is to do with our body's cells. Each one has consciousness and this consciousness is responsive to our inner activities, attitudes, expectations, thoughts and feelings. Our bodies are made of exquisitely sensitive, reactive and dynamic material. We are not dead-skin bags filled with inert lumps of meat and bone. Every one of our trillions of cells is highly charged. All of them are interacting with our living processes through their own consciousness. And the *Inner Smile Meditation* enables us to influence that consciousness and harness it for our benefit. Also, people who are kind, considerate, accepting and available to their bodies are generally much healthier, happier people.

Exercise 1: How You Approach Your Body. What about you? How do you treat your body? Consider the following questions:

- Do you expect your body to work for long hours without rest or recognition?
- Do you thank it for what it has done for you for years?
- Do you ignore it almost completely?
- Do you feel gratitude for the way it serves you?
- Do you criticise and demand more of it, no matter what?
- Do you offer help and healing when it hurts, or gets sick?
- Do you nurture and protect it as you would a little child in your care?

Briefly note your answers in your logbook.

The *Inner Smile Meditation* enables us to act differently, if we need to, by helping to heal past damage and prompting us to take better care of our bodies. The moment we give warm recognition and love to our bodies, they begin to open, to relax, to heal, to thrive, and to develop strength and resilience once more. Our contractedness reverses. With bodily expansion, our feeling and thinking lives expand, too. We become more open and alive in all areas, including during meditation.

BENEFITS WHEN MEDITATING

Meditation doesn't magically suspend our habitual ways of feeling, thinking and behaving. While meditating, therefore, we are likely to experience whatever we encounter at other times. Moreover, because meditation is a very stimulating, life-enhancing process, we are more inclined to experience intensity as we meditate. *The Inner Smile Meditation* helps us to deal with this intensity, whatever its nature. It adds a soothing, healing dimension to the process through its effects in us.

SHORT INNER SMILE MEDITATION

You can do this meditation briefly or for as long you want.

Meditation 1: Brief Inner Smile Meditation. Sit or stand comfortably. Pay attention to the contact of your body with what is supporting you so you are well grounded. Then centre yourself briefly, too. Next, pay attention to different parts of your body. In the beginning, choose parts that are comfortable or more comfortable than other parts. As you pay attention to each of them, align with your observer and smile at them through your inner eyes. Embrace them with warmth and affection and keep smiling until you get a return smile or warmth. Then move on to other parts. Alternatively, you can smile at the whole or major parts of your body at one time. Note your reactions in your logbook.

FULL INNER SMILE MEDITATION

We start the *Full Inner Smile Meditation* in our eyes. During the meditation, we internally look at, listen to or feel the various parts of our bodies, including our smiling eyes themselves. We imagine developing connections between our smiling eyes and whatever they are paying attention to. Using this connection as a medium, we cultivate affectionate, loving, smiling, exchanges and sharing.

Meditation 2: Full Inner Smile Meditation.

Step 1: Sit comfortably and get yourself grounded and centred by noticing the contact of your body with what is supporting you and by aligning with your observer – your sense of self.

Step 2: As you sit there, notice your eyes. Allow them to soften. Imagine they are like clear windows through which you are looking. Imagine they are bathed in a loving balm that leaves them feeling relaxed, clear, quiet, sweet and fresh. Keep doing this until you can experience softening, brightening, quietening or sweetening in your eyes.

Step 3: As you keep meditating on your eyes like this, encourage the effects of what you are doing to spread. Gradually allow the softness, transparency, quietness and sweetness to seep down your face through your cheeks. Keep encouraging it until the whole front of your face is completely saturated with the sensations from your eyes. When these sensations reach your mouth, allow its corners to curl up a little. If you notice your eyes wanting to close slightly or completely during the process, allow them to do this.

Step 4: Now, physically smile with your eyes. Squeeze the muscles in the corners of your eyes very slightly so that small smile lines appear. Just a hint is fine. To heighten the effect as you do this, you can imagine each eye is like a face that has its own smiling eyes and mouth. Encourage your mouth to smile as well and allow toothy grins, even laughter to follow!

Step 5: Also allow yourself to experience the pleasure of your smile in all of your senses. Let this pleasure keep going all the way down the front of your body; encouraging it to spread up from there to fill all of you: front, back, top, bottom, midline and body wall. Do this for several minutes.

Step 6: Now, turn your attention to specific parts of your body. As you do, smile with tenderness, love and acceptance at each of those parts, and keep smiling until you experience them joining you and sharing your smile. If it helps, imagine that each body part is a person (a child, perhaps) who is open and vulnerable, responsive to you and happy that you are smiling at it. Imagine that it wants to join in with you. The goal is to share a loving, tender smile with every part of your body and with your body as a whole. As you continue with this, notice any distinctive changes that accompany the moments of sharing that occur.

Step 7: Keep doing the meditation for as long as you have time. And when you finish make brief notes about your experience in your logbook. Make a plan to repeat this meditation as soon as you can.

BODY CLENCHING

Experiments show that clenching the dominant side of the body helps to produce a sense of security, lightness, openness and optimism.

You clench the right-hand side if you are a 'right hander' and the left-hand side if you are a 'left hander'. You can choose for yourself if you are ambidextrous. Clenching simply involves tightening up the muscles. Interestingly, clenching the sub-dominant side tends to produce the opposite effects.

One of the simplest ways of clenching during meditation is to clench your dominant hand into a fist. You can do this several times. The effects of this process seem to arise in the bedrock of our bodies and seem to be more generalised than the inner smile meditation. A wonderful sense of security and wellbeing, even serenity, is stimulated as we persist, even at times when we are experiencing significant discomfort. Experiment and find out what you notice.

Meditation 3: Inner Smile and Clenching.

Step 1: Sit or stand comfortably. Keep yourself grounded and centred by noticing the contact of your body with what is supporting you and by aligning with your observer. Keep doing this until you are settled and present with the meditation. Clench your fist a few times as you do this. Keep clenching your fist from time to time during the rest of the meditation. Clench the right hand if you are right-handed and the left hand if you are left-handed; clench either if you are ambidextrous.

Step 2: Now, beginning in your eyes, smile. You can do this by squeezing the muscles in the corners of your eyes so that your smile lines appear very slightly.. Just a hint is fine. Or, if this does not help you to smile easily, remember someone whom you like; imagine this person is in front of you smiling at you, and imagine that you are smiling at him or her.

Step 3: Let the smile stay in your eyes for a while and then gradually allow it to spread to your mouth too, if it is not already smiling. It is fine for this to be a light smile, or more intense if you want it to be. Allow yourself to experience the pleasure of the smile through all your senses. Clench your fist a few more times.

Step 4: Practise paying attention to the aspects of your experience that you would like to intensify. Notice the effects of what you are doing. When you stop, make brief notes in your logbook. Decide when you will do this meditation again.

28
Opening Our Hearts

'When our hearts are filled with love,
our heads are filled with light.'
(Author unknown)

An open heart is fundamental to finding inspiration from the Infinite (see Chapter 1). Our hearts are also fundamental to our feeling and spiritual lives. Like blood carrying life-giving substances to every part of our bodies, our heart-felt feelings and energies carry essential emotional nutrients and healing ingredients into every part of our beings.

Many of us are strongly cerebral these days, however, which can inhibit the nutritional value of our feelings reaching their destinations. We have been taught from early in life to concentrate on thinking and rational processing, and this is important. Raw data, facts and logic are essential in life. We need to learn how to use them in making our decisions and guiding what we do. Thinking clearly is also central to imagining goals, goal-setting and effective decision-making (see Chapters 5, 6 and 24).

However, information and fact-based living alone can be calculating, cold and hard. This does not make them wrong; but living mainly like this can be very one-sided. There is more to life than facts, more than logic and rationality.

Love, nurturing and tenderness are fundamental too, and these are about promoting growth, connectedness, joining, cooperation, respect, resolving differences, healing wounds and many other things. Our heart-felt feelings also add the juice of satisfaction and fulfilment to the emotionally desiccated realms of pure rationality.

We can discover all of this as we open ourselves emotionally and experience the enlivening effects that come to us from heart-felt exchanges. We can discover that our hearts are exquisitely perceptive organs for processing reality, just as our brains are; only they do it differently. In fact, we can discover that the combination of 'our hearts and our heads' produces a balance not possible from using either one alone.

Meditation 1: Opening Our Hearts. Get yourself grounded by paying attention to the physical aspects of your experience, both inside and outside your body. Then centre in your physical heart by seeing yourself there, feeling yourself there, hearing yourself there, and talking to yourself about being there (see Chapter 12). After doing this for a short time, meditate that beautiful, loving, pink, warm, mellow, melodious heart energy begins to fill you, flooding you with its delicious sweetness. As you see, hear, feel and taste this energy spreading through your body, repeat the words, 'I-Am love' over and over, like a mantra. Notice what happens and record any changes in your logbook.

LOVE

To open our hearts, all we need to do is to concentrate on them from time to time. As we do, we energise them and promote the release of love in them, a feeling always waiting in there. (Remember the principles of centring in Chapter 12.) Love is a deliciously sweet energy that opens our eyes to the beauty of all creation and fills us with warmth and joy. Love is a healing and uniting force in the world. It melts away discord. Love begets love; and can open us to love in all its other forms. The experience of love can be physical, emotional, cognitive and spiritual: called *body love*, *feeling love*, *person love* and *being love.*[46]

Most importantly, love is the foundation of everything that is. As we awaken spiritually, we discover this; we discover that love is Life and dwells in the source of Life from which we all arise. We discover that as well as a feeling, love is a state of being that we experience and know through our blissful union with I-Am and the Infinite.

Principle 1: Love and union are one; love produces union and union produces love.

Using this principle we can experience union with people by cultivating feelings of love for them; and we can feel love for people by moving into union with them. We can also do both together. We often have direct experiences of this when with babies and young children, and when we are in love with someone.

Meditation 2: Love and Union. Sit comfortably and bring a person (or other living creature) you love into your awareness. Imagine as vividly, fully and strongly as you can that you are with him or her. See, feel, hear, taste or smell him or her together with you. Maybe talk about this to yourself as well. Then feel the love you share with him or her and imagine you are blending together with each other. Notice the experiences you have as you do this. In particular, notice how the love and the union support one another. Record what you notice in your logbook when you stop.

Exercise 1: Promoting Open-Heartedness with Others. We can do many simple things in our daily lives to activate our hearts:

- Hug people or animals regularly.
- Smile at others and say affectionate things, such as, 'I love you' or 'I care for you'.
- Do things for others that we have not been asked to do; and do them for the joy of doing them.
- Use words like 'tenderness', 'cherish', 'love', 'like', 'adore', 'care for' and 'fond of'…
- Say often, 'I feel…'
- Say often, 'I love you', 'I love that…' and 'I loved going to…'
- Spend at least a few minutes a day cherishing your loved ones in your thoughts and actions.
- Fantasise love at every opportunity; remember loving times.
- List the most loving experiences you have had; remember that the fragrances associated with past experiences reawaken the original intensity.
- Keep your physical heart in your awareness as you go about your daily life.
- Regularly cherish yourself with the mantra 'I-Am love'.
- Change your environment: surround yourself with loving colours, sounds, textures, tastes and smells.

The more often you do these things, the stronger their momentum will become in your life. And the stronger this momentum is, the easier it will be to maintain your loving orientation. Make notes in your logbook of any changes you notice over the weeks, months and years ahead.

Once started on this path, we quickly discover how our capacity to love others is determined by our capacity to love ourselves.

And these capacities come directly from how well loved we were as children. Whatever our beginnings were, however, whether loving or not, we can quickly learn to embrace ourselves more fully with love and thereby enhance our capacities to love others as well. Remember, the bedrock of who we are – I-Am and the Infinite – is pure love.

Meditation 3: Loving Ourselves. Spend a few minutes each day sitting comfortably and thinking about you. Include the way you look, the way you act, your favourite qualities and features, your least favourite qualities and features… anything and everything that comes into your awareness. As you do this, pay attention to your physical heart and embrace these qualities by saying, 'I love you.' Do this as if you are communicating with a small child whom you are cherishing, nurturing, protecting and loving. Whether or not you feel the love initially, keep repeating, 'I love you' until you experience love or at least some softening. Remember to stay grounded and centred while doing this. Make notes in your log-book at the end.

We can do exactly the same meditation with other people and discover that we can intensify the love we already feel towards them or, if we don't feel that way, that the meditation can still change things for the better. It helps to unify us with others, which in turn helps us to join with them, instead of polarising away from them (see Chapter 23).

INFINITE LOVE

The foundation of all things, love arises in the Infinite. Love is Life Itself. Love is in everything that we know and can know. It is the primal energy from which everything arises. Maybe these thoughts or suggestions are not familiar to you, or seem like wild fantasies, yet love is always here for us to experience and know.

We can become transported when we experience love directly and discover that there is much more to life than the tug and pull of everyday events. And notice what love does to the facts, data and information we gather through our senses. *Love turns facts into wisdom.* As love saturates our information about others, our world, and ourselves, our perceptions align with Life Itself, beautifully transforming all that we know. The Ancients seem to have known this, because they taught that the heart is the seat of the soul. The simple meditations and exercises in this chapter give us an opportunity to investigate this teaching for ourselves, to discover that our hearts are the portals through which passion and compassion enter our lives.

As our hearts open and expand, we find other qualities and capacities also expand, including intuition, perceptiveness and our capacity for inspiration. We discover aspects of ourselves we didn't know existed. We also become open to many amazing realms as part of the awakening process. Poets, mystics and storytellers have understood this through the ages. As time passes, keep notes in your logbook of the differences you notice in you.

29
MANTRA MEDITATION

'What's your father doing?' a teenager was asked by a visiting friend who wanted to talk with him.
'Oh, he's meditating in the other room.'
'Meditating?' the visitor questioned.
'Yes,' she answered with a playful grin, 'he's got his legs tied in knots on the floor and he's saying, "Ningg, ningg, ningg, ningg..."'

Mantras are powerful tools for the awakening of consciousness and for the realisation of our full potential as human beings. As part of producing these results, they also have a profound influence on our capacity to manage everyday life. Used for many thousands of years, there are probably millions of mantras.

The results that come from a particular mantra depend on the mantra itself. One way to understand this is to think of mantra repetition as being like using a remote control to a TV set. We select a number (repeat a mantra) and gain access to a particular channel (experiences and knowing revealed by the mantra). Given time and repeated viewings (continued mantra repetition), we observe and experience what is available through that channel (the range associated with the mantra). Using different mantras is like pressing different buttons on the remote in order to open us to different types of knowing and experiencing.

The mantra we introduce in this chapter enables us to harvest the full fruits of our other practices. Perhaps amongst the most profound practices of them all, it embraces all levels of being and enables us to know and live the transcendent beauty, fulfilment and understanding inherent in Life at its very roots – the Infinite. In other words, as wonderful and powerful as all the other techniques and practices are, this mantra meditation is more. It floods us with the fulfilment and completion of Life itself.

Known by some as the *Vedic Mantra,* its use promotes awakening and enlightenment. We have discussed these outcomes earlier in the book in terms of 'full alignment with I-Am' and 'being the Infinite'. Many of us also use this mantra because of its practical

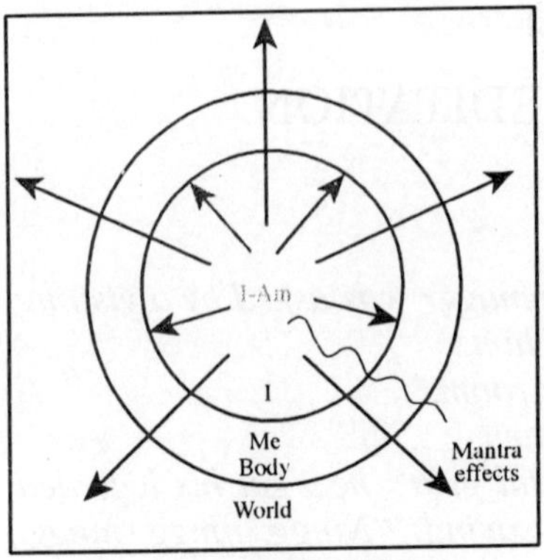

Mantra Awakens Us from World to 'I-Am' and the 'Infinite'

benefits. As we repeat it, the words simultaneously tune us into different aspects of our awareness and consciousness, progressively opening us to the direct experience of both worldly and ultimate levels of reality, and increasing the life energy available in our systems. As the mantra produces these changes, it also aligns us physically, emotionally, mentally and spiritually with the Infinite.

Combined with the *Grounding Meditation* and the *Centring Meditation*, the *Vedic Mantra Meditation* has an even more profound impact on us than when it is done alone.

Grounding ensures that we are earthed physically in the world, and that we stay balanced, clear and pure; centring enables us to plug fully into the life energy of the Infinite and receive the enlivening, healing, fulfilling and awakening benefits that doing so carries. Repeating the Vedic Mantra directly increases the flow of that life energy through our systems, making us whole.

Clearly, given these wonderful effects, the *Vedic Mantra Meditation* is marvellously rewarding. When we think of how little is involved in the actual process – simply repeating the words – it is a miracle that so much can come from doing so little.

SPIRITUAL BENEFITS

Many spiritual benefits arise from this mantra. For example:

- It is a tool for directly promoting spiritual awakening.
- High-intensity experiences of Life increase, resulting in increasing light, brilliance, effulgence, joy, love, bliss, peace, quietness, harmony, sweetness, purity and essence.
- The Vedic Mantra arises in the source of Life, the Infinite, and whenever we repeat it, that source can reveal itself to us in our greater sense of presence.

A short list of worldly outcomes includes:

- Energy and vitality
- Clarity of thinking and purpose
- Understanding
- Confidence and hope
- Resolution of past problems
- Physical, emotional and mental healing
- Inner strength and resilience
- Distilling and releasing the past
- Delighting in life
- Joy, love, brightness and harmony
- Abiding fulfilment
- Expanded worldly consciousness
- A deep sense of coming home at last
- Sensitivity to others

WHAT MANTRAS ARE

Mantras are words: from one to many words. Some mantras are so long, in fact, that they take hours to say once. They can be used to promote many outcomes, including the support of health, building inner strength, releasing the past, making money, strengthening our capacity for love, and expanding awakened consciousness.

Another approach is for us to think of mantras as *words of power* that transform our lives through their direct influence. How does this work? Well, think of the way different sounds affect us: some are soothing and relaxing, some are discordant and disturbing, some are invigorating and stimulating, some are brightening and transporting. Also, thinking of the principle *what we notice is what we get*, enables us to realise the power of our consciousness (see Chapter 6). Mantras help reshape and redirect all of this.

INITIATION

The most powerful introduction to any mantra is through initiation by a master of that mantra (see Chapter 34). A master of a mantra is someone who has realised the significant outcomes of using that mantra. The initiation begins or intensifies an unfolding process in the recipient, a process that will be catalysed by the master's level of realisation from then on. This initiation accelerates many aspects of the awakening that the mantra offers.

> *I've been initiated in a variety of ways and have often experienced immediate effects. I particularly remember a beautiful experience with Thakur, a master whom we visited regularly in*

Kolkata over a period of nine years. I was turned slightly towards him, sitting on the floor beside, and slightly in front of, his chair. I looked up at him as he was speaking. Radiant with love, he unexpectedly looked down at me, reached out and touched me under my chin – a quick touch that lingered slightly before he turned away again. I was left with cascading tingles streaming down from my chin into my chest and heart. Transported by the unfolding effects that followed, I knew he had just initiated me again.

The way initiations are done varies. The particular style and type of realisation of the initiator leads to these variations. It may be done:

- By a master saying the sound into our ears (traditional way).
- Through audio or visual recordings or the equivalent.
- Through a look or touch.
- In writing via letter, email, SMS, etc.
- Telepathically without any overt or obvious exchange.

Telepathic methods are possible for those meditation masters who can meditate people into awakened states from a distance.

MANTRA MEDITATION

The practice of mantra meditation involves repeating the words over and over, and cultivating self-aware attention as we do. That is, as we repeat the mantra we remain aware both of what we are doing and that we are doing it (see Chapter 8). The repetition of the words is what produces the results. Just how this occurs will become clear as we continue to meditate. Of course, part of the challenge is to sustain our attention on the mantra repetition.

HOW TO REPEAT THE MANTRA

We can repeat mantras in many different ways and these variations make a difference to the results we get. For example, as well as saying the mantra aloud, we may internally repeat it by seeing the words repeating, actually hearing the words repeating (which is different from inner talking), feeling their repetition somewhere in our bodies, or by tasting or smelling the repetition. (Yes, some people do this!)

Your natural capacities are your best guide to what to do here: visual people will see the mantra, auditory people will hear it, kinaesthetic people will feel it, people who talk to themselves will say it internally, and gustatory and olfactory people will taste and smell it. Experiment if you are uncertain what is easiest for you. Combining approaches works well too.

COMMON STAGES IN MANTRA REPETITION

For most people, mantra repetition starts off as a technique that they are told is good for them. However, although told this, at the beginning we can experience the repetition as meaningless, ritualistic, boring or pointless. We may only do it because we hope for the promised results, not because we are getting them or know we will. What great advertising this is!

By contrast, some people do have wonderful experiences from the very first. Hopefully this will be you. Such experiences may continue for a while or be one-off events. Whatever their frequency or duration, our desire to repeat these experience can become a trap, because the hope that we will tends to get in the way.

Our best response is to meditate intently on what we are experiencing in each moment and to let go of comparisons (see Chapters 13 and 30). Otherwise our meditations can become an exercise in frustration: wanting something that we do not have, or trying to turn what we have into something we once had but have no more. Some people spend years trying to do this before realising its futility: the first experience is already past and no longer available in its original form.

In the next stage, our understanding expands as we realise that our repetition also involves the experiences we have while repeating the words. Whether we are aware of it or not, change occurs as we persist with our repetition, and with this change comes shifts of perception. We eventually understand that our experiences as we repeat the words are the mantra too, that there is no separation between them and the mantra. So mantra meditation can be today's shopping list, yesterday's argument, the plan for tomorrow's events…everything we think, feel, remember or experience as we repeat the words. And gradually, as the words and our experiences start to become one, the nature of our repetition changes too.

During what often follows, we begin to understand and increasingly to realise that the mantra is a means of knowing Life itself, of aligning with I-Am and the Infinite. We begin to experience directly that the mantra operates in us at different densities, that it energises us at all levels and that it opens us and cleanses us at all levels, too. Eventually, we 'know the mantra in everything', even when its presence is sometimes so subtle that we could miss it if we aren't alert. This stage accompanies an advanced process of exploration that was not available earlier.

Note: I recommend that you avoid trying to fit your experience into the above stages. They highlight general tendencies only which give a little taste of some of the possibilities. Your unfolding experience of mantra meditation could be very different.

MANTRA MEDITATIONS

Meditation 1: Vedic Mantra Meditation.[47] Sit or stand comfortably. Get yourself grounded and centred. Then repeat the Vedic mantra, *Om Tat Sat*. Do this for at least two minutes and for as long as you decide to do it if you want to take more time. Notice what occurs as you do and record your observations in your logbook.[48] You can also use another mantra. You may already have been initiated, for example, or you could choose words like 'Love', 'God', 'nature', 'fulfilment', 'I-Am', 'the Infinite' or something else that has a natural appeal to you.

30
THE AWAKENING MEDITATION

The awakening meditation is a wonderful spiritual practice that uses many of the techniques already introduced. It is deeply transforming and enlightening. It promotes the awakening of consciousness, the fulfilment of our spiritual destinies, and it opens us to participation with the Infinite. At the same time, we discover how the reclaiming of our animal natures is a royal road to awakening. In other words, we become deeply aware of our bodies and their influence on every moment of our lives. We discover how living life with I-Am and the Infinite as our centre, and being grounded in and caring for our bodies and the planet, enable us to realise the spiritual purposes that we yearn to fulfil.

Meditation 1: The Awakening Meditation. This meditation is an integration of seven steps, each one a meditation in itself, that make a unique contribution to our awakening. They complement each other, producing more than the specific results of each one.

Step 1: Noticing. With noticing, we cultivate awareness of everything. We remain alert and attentive to what is occurring inside and around us. Awareness is primary in spiritual awakening. We start by looking around and seeing what is there; listening to the sounds and hearing them clearly; feeling the pressure of our bodies on what is supporting them, our clothing on our skin, the temperature of the air; and noticing any tastes and smells. At the same time, we notice what is going on inside us – our thoughts, feelings, impulses, desires, memories, especially noticing our physical sensations: heat, cold, tingling, ease, tension, fatigue, pain, contraction, openness (see Chapter 13). Along with this dual noticing, we notice any sensate linkages, exchanges or connectedness between our bodily sensations and our awareness of the world around us.

Step 2: Accepting. With accepting, we practise acknowledging what is occurring inside and around us. Instead of censoring, filtering, distorting, minimising, or exaggerating whatever we notice so it fits what suits us, what we like or what we are comfortable with, we accept its presence, welcoming it and remaining open to it as it is. Remaining open to the reality of inner and outer awareness is fundamental in spiritual awakening. We accept whatever is in our awareness; in particular, we accept its presence inside or around us. We affirm, 'I accept you' and 'I welcome you'. We recognise its presence, like nodding to a friend who has just arrived (see Chapter 13).

Step 3: Experiencing. Experiencing involves embracing and living the reality of our physical perceptions and our bodily sensations. Ensuring that we fully experience and know what occurs inside and around us is necessary to spiritual awakening. Without the full experience, we will not have awakening. While remaining alert and aware, and accepting our experience, we need to live the full intensity of what is there, whether it is mild or strong. In particular, it is the full physical experience of what we are noticing and accepting that we encourage. Whatever is there becomes more than something we are experiencing or observing; we *become* the experience by meditating that we are immersed in it, saturated in it and at one with it (see Chapter 13).

Step 4: Grounding. Grounding brings us into the here-and-now and digests our experiences. This nourishes us, and creates physical, emotional, cognitive and spiritual balance and equilibrium. It harnesses all our experiences, purifies our consciousness and opens us to awakening. Importantly, it releases our systems to digest the remnants of our past experiences, resolving and healing as it does. While continuing the first three steps, we pay close sensate attention to our physical sensations, the world around us, and their connections within us. If this seems to distract us from our meditation, we accept this distraction. Persistence brings light, harmony, ease, sweetness and fragrance (see Chapters 9 and 10).

Step 5: Centring. Centring opens us to I-Am, our ultimate sense of self, and our source of Life – the Infinite. It produces awareness of self and enables us to experience and align with this. With grounding, this brings us into the I-Am-here-and-now in which awareness of I-Am can arise and full awakening becomes possible. As we continue to ground ourselves, we discover the faculty – the sense of self – in us that is witnessing or observing our experiences. This self may be 'inside' our experience, encompass it, or be it. We cultivate self-aware attention to experience this observer and, whatever its nature, we become that, identifying with it fully (see Chapters 8, 11 and 12).

Step 6: Cherishing. Cherishing creates oneness, wholeness and healing in our systems, and paves the way for the state of union that is required for realising I-Am and oneness in the Infinite.

It uses the power of love to do this. While practising grounding and centring, we centre in our hearts and cultivate increasing warmth, light, sweetness and grace-filled energy in there. To promote these outcomes we can also do the *Inner Smile* and *Body Clenching Meditations* (see Chapter 27). The opening of our hearts gradually softens, melds, heals and makes everything one (see Chapter 28). We embrace all our experiences with love, nurturing, tenderness, gratitude and appreciation. We cherish and welcome everything.

Step 7: Divining. Divining floods our systems with spiritual energy, perception, knowing, healing and awakening. Using words, symbols or activities of power (mantras, yantras/mandalas, or physical practices), we realise I-Am and our participation in the Infinite. Divining expands our everyday capacity for transcendent-awakened oneness. *The Vedic Mantra Meditation* or other suitable mantras are ideal. Whatever we choose, our practice opens us to absorption with the Infinite from which all our practices arise.

Step 8: Overall Practice: Guiding. We need to keep to our overall intention as we take the previous steps, a need made all the more important because there are seven of them. To do this, we need to monitor and manage our meditation in order to encourage a state of overall integration, oneness and awakening. This monitoring prompts us to keep doing all seven steps and at times to increase our emphasis on any specific steps that we have allowed to lapse temporarily. The result is a deliberate, ongoing shifting of primary emphasis on and between the seven steps, a process that opens us to the full awakening that is available to us through them.

Regularly make notes about your experiences in your logbook as you keep doing this meditation.

31
INTEGRATING MEDITATION INTO EVERYDAY LIFE

A regular meditation practice is a lot easier when we make practical arrangements for it to be a comfortable part of our lives. Several suggestions are discussed in this chapter, including:

- When to meditate.
- How long and how often to meditate.
- Where to meditate.
- Postures and positions.
- Moving and meditation.
- The use of music.
- The value of exercise.

WHEN TO MEDITATE

Time is precious. Work and home pressures are ever present and fitting extras into our lives is often challenging. So, clearly, making time for meditation could require some adjustments. However, once we get started, the fundamental nourishment meditation provides can make it a high priority in our lives. But the first thing is to start.

Choose a time that suits your regular program. Ideally find times that are as free from interruptions as possible. In the beginning, choosing a fixed time is often helpful. This helps to establish a habit with the time itself becoming a natural reminder.

Choose times that suit you temperamentally. Most of us find some times much more practical, satisfying or beneficial than others – for example, the beginning, middle or end of the day.

Use day-to-day incidents to prompt you to meditate. They could include particular events, feelings, time intervals, people, tasks, or situations. Be specific about what you choose.

HOW LONG AND HOW OFTEN TO MEDITATE

Meditate at least once a day and stop all other activities to do this. This helps us to deal with the pressures of life. Stopping all outer activity and going inside in order to become settled is imperative. Our in-built healing and self-sustaining capacities need these times. Even so, many people find this challenging because of the internal adjustments that are necessary as we start to meditate. Many of us rarely stop these days, even for a few minutes, without something external to do. We watch TV, read, answer emails or text messages, talk to others…

Just Sitting

We need to get used to just sitting without something external to do. Stopping our physical activities helps us to stop on the inside, too. And it gets easier as our old patterns subside, replaced by inner tranquillity, freedom, clarity, quietness and peace.

> *After many years of working very long hours, seven days a week, I finally understood the cost of this to my health and to me as a person. So I made space in my life – just to sit. But in the beginning, instead of the peace and ease I expected, my thoughts kept racing about. At times, without noticing, I would be on my feet to go back to work. The solution came when I made a definite decision to keep sitting no matter what tricks I got up to internally to avoid doing so. Succeeding at this was the best thing I did in my life.*

Meditation 1: Stopping by Using Grounding and Centring. Sit in a comfortable position and concentrate on grounding and centring. (See Chapters 9 to 12 for specific instructions.) Let your thoughts, feelings, memories, desires, impulses, etc – whatever is there – prompt awareness of your body and what you are experiencing physically. Everything will gradually subside as you persist with this practice. Make notes in your logbook of what you experience.

Choosing How Long

At the beginning, choose to meditate for a time that you know you will complete. Five to ten minutes is often suitable, or even less. Make a deliberate decision to complete this time, no matter what.

Increase your time when you have become well accustomed to meditating for that long. Only make the increases gradually – say at the rate of a few minutes each week. By increasing slowly, we accustom ourselves to what we are doing a little at a time, which makes the necessary internal and external adjustments easier.

Useful Precautions

People can meditate too much. We need to maintain a balance between our everyday lives and our meditation practices.

Ensure that you continue to take care of your day-to-day needs and obligations. We need to avoid neglecting our basic health, family, work and other everyday responsibilities.

Meditate for no more than an hour a day in the early years; and divide this time into at least two sessions. These comments don't apply to meditations like grounding, which help us to connect more fully to the world around us and to our daily lives. The more we do these ones, the better.

How Often to Meditate

Meditating regularly is usually best; however, any meditation is helpful, so every time we do it – even intermittently – we receive benefits. All the same, regular meditation helps us build up a momentum in our practice. Carried by this, the benefits from each session will last increasingly longer between sessions, until the benefits from the last one overlap with the start of the next one.

Meditating at least twice a day will help to spread the benefits.

Keeping to Your Times

We can make some simple arrangements to ensure we meditate as planned. For example:

- Let others know when we will be unavailable.
- Make sure that we keep ourselves free for our meditation times: put a red line through these times in our organisers.
- Pause and remember the important reasons we are meditating when tempted to give something else a higher priority.

WHERE TO MEDITATE

It is possible to meditate almost anywhere. However, some places may not suit you in the beginning, so it makes sense to find locations in which you can meditate as easily and peacefully as possible. At the same time, it is worthwhile eventually learning to deal with distractions so you can meditate regardless of what is going on around you.

Preparing the Surroundings

Make your meditation place special. It's a good idea to choose somewhere attractive and appealing, or to beautify it yourself. This will add to your pleasure whenever you are there.

Consecrating the meditation area helps to mark its importance. Dedicating your area solely to your meditation practice helps. You can do this in several ways. Think of how you would like the area to look, your preferred music, the lighting, pictures, fragrances and temperature. Do small rituals at the beginning of each session to foster its specialness – light incense, say an affirmation, put on special music, etc.

Dedicate certain things exclusively for your meditation. For example, you could include a silk-covered cushion, meditation beads, 'spiritual' music, photos of significant people, incense, important books or texts, or special clothing.

When your space is shared, use things that are easily portable. This enables you to bring them in and remove them without effort.

Notice how the places and items you use regularly become charged with meditative energy. The locations and objects we use develop a special kind of aura that becomes more intense as our practices mature. When this meditative charge becomes strong enough, the energy alone can stimulate us into meditative states.

Preparing Others

Tell others what you are doing and ask them to leave you alone until you are finished. You can also take sensible precautions such as putting on an answering machine, turning off your mobile phone, and putting up a sign, e.g., 'Available again at 2.30.'

POSTURE AND POSITIONS

Posture is very important in meditation. Comfort is also important, and our bodies need time to adjust to unfamiliar postures and positions. The fastest way to master any new posture is to practise a little of what is required first, then gradually extend what we do.

The first thing to learn is that keeping the spine and neck straight contributes a lot. A straight spine and neck encourages the flow of 'meditative' energy through the body.

Choosing a Posture or Position

The following postures are all good for meditation and it is usually best to start with one that you find comfortable. Remember to take account of your physical condition as you make your selection. For example, if you have arthritis or any injuries, choose a posture that provides enough support to avoid aggravating anything. Also, you can use pillows, folded rugs or something similar to support your body in any way that you need.

Sitting on a Chair

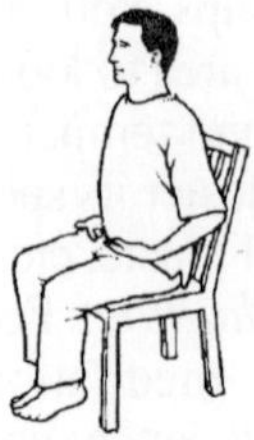

Sitting on a chair is good for almost everyone. Preferably choose a straight-backed chair. Sit forward on the seat so you can stay upright without leaning, although you can lean if you need to. Have your feet flat on the floor or resting on something if your legs are too short. Many low, comfortable chairs are better for sleep than meditation!

Kneeling

We can kneel in many different ways. 'Good knees' help with this! You can make the process easier by kneeling on something soft like a cushion, a folded rug or thick carpet.

Kneeling stools: These enable you to sit as you kneel, making the posture easier. They raise your buttocks off the floor, take the weight off your lower legs and reduce the tension in your knees.

Saddles: These are a variation on stools. A bulky cushion or other object is placed on the floor. You then kneel astride this and lower your weight onto it, as if riding a horse. The height and width of the 'saddle' are chosen for comfort, particularly for the spread of your knees and the height of your buttocks off the floor.

Cushions or folded rugs: Kneeling with a cushion or folded rug placed flat between the buttocks and the lower legs is very comfortable for some people. You'll need good knees for this.

Cross-legged Sitting

Three cross-legged positions are traditional and frequently used in many parts of the world.

The easy position: You get into this one by sitting on the floor or something soft with your legs straight out in front of you. You then bend your legs, crossing them at the shins and pull them in so the sides of both feet are on the floor. The back and neck are kept as straight as possible, although keeping the lower back straight in this position is a challenge.

The half lotus position: This position is more physically demanding than the first. To get into it, you sit with your legs straight out in front of you. You then bend one leg (left/right), putting the sole of the foot against the underside of the

other thigh (right/left), with the side of the foot on the floor. Then you bend the other leg (right/left), putting the foot on top of the thigh of the first leg (left/right) so the heel is on or near the groin. The calf of the bottom leg lies along the floor, with the calf of the top leg lying on top of it. The legs don't cross as they do in the previous posture. The back and neck are held straight.

The full lotus position: This position is an extension of the half lotus position. It requires even more suppleness and almost certainly more time for practice to become comfortable. You get into it by sitting with your legs straight out in front you. You then bend the right leg and place the foot on top of the left thigh. The heel of the right foot is near the left groin, possibly in contact with the pelvic bone. You allow the ankle to bend so the sole of the foot faces up. You then bend the left leg at the knee and place its foot on top of the right thigh with its heel close to the right groin. Each foot is then resting on the top of the thigh of the other leg with the heel in contact with the groin. Your shins cross near the ankles. The back and neck are held straight.

Sitting on Firm Round Cushions: This very simple device makes cross-legged sitting much easier. When in any of the other cross-legged positions, you can place a thick cushion under the buttocks. This opens out the angle between the torso and the thighs and reduces the tension in the lower back and groins.

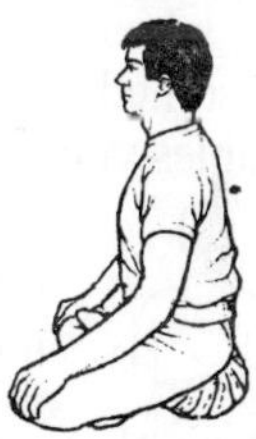

Lying/Prone Positions

Stretching out to meditate on the floor, on a bed, or on some other comfortable surface is very attractive at times. This is particularly true if you are tired or have physical problems that are eased by lying down. As with some of the other positions, added comfort is possible with the selective use of cushions, pillows and rugs. Three positions work well.

Lying flat on the back: You lie on your back with your arms on the floor at your sides. You place your hands slightly out from your thighs. You can also place your hands on your belly or chest, one on top of the other. These hand positions are good for building up energy. You can cross your legs at the ankles as well, if energy retention is important. Placing pillows under the knees takes pressure off the lower spine and the knees. Placing suitably shaped pillows under the head, neck and upper back is also helpful for keeping the spine and neck straight, and to avoid jamming the chin onto the throat. Using other well-placed cushions or pillows, you can also support your arms and elbows.

Lying on the right side: Some Taoist and Tibetan Buddhist practitioners recommend this in preference to lying on the back. You lie on the right side with the right leg fairly straight. You support your right cheek and ear with the palm of the right hand, bend the left leg at the knee and hook the left foot over the right calf about halfway up. The left arm rests along the top of the left side and thigh. Using a pillow to support the head is often helpful to ensure the neck and back are straight. Another pillow or cushion placed under the left knee can help take pressure off the left hip if necessary.

Lying on the left side: Some Taoist practitioners recommend against this position. However, it is helpful for people who can neither lie on their backs, nor their right sides. It is the mirror image of the previous one.

Standing Positions

Standing enables you to take advantage of short periods during the day when you have a few moments to stand, maybe while waiting for something. The natural uprightness you have in this position often enables you to be more relaxed and alert than in other positions.

Relaxed standing: Stay as relaxed as possible when standing erect. Place your feet about shoulder width apart, or a little closer together if that is more comfortable. Adjust the spine and neck so they are in alignment. Position your head so that you are looking ahead 'straight and level'; and allow your arms to dangle slackly at your sides.

Stressed standing: This position is useful at times, particularly when you need to stay aware of your body, or when grounding or centring. To get into this position, first move into the relaxed standing position. Then, turn your toes in slightly, bend your knees until you feel tension in your thighs, and twist your legs outwards at the knees. While holding your legs in this position, spread your arms so your hands are about a foot (30 centimetres) out from each side. Maintain this position.

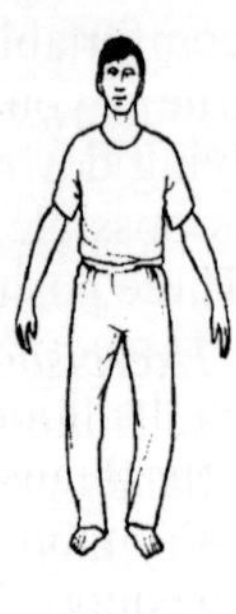

Mobile 'Positions'

You may be surprised to learn that you can meditate while moving around, too: walking, running, roller-blading, swimming, bicycle riding, gardening, skiing, skating, sailing, climbing, cleaning the bath, vacuum cleaning – just to name a few.

Exercise 1: Postural Adjustment. Choose a posture that you wish to master. Begin by gently getting into that posture as much as you can. Do this each time you start to meditate. While learning, maintain the posture for a short time (perhaps only seconds); then release yourself from it. Stretch and relax briefly, then go through the sequence again, holding the posture you have chosen for a short while. Then again release yourself and stretch and relax briefly. Repeat this sequence several more times. Make notes of what you notice in your logbook.

Hand Positions

Known as *mudras* in yoga, hand positions have a significant impact on our experiences while we meditate. In fact, this is another vast area that has been investigated by practitioners for millennia. To begin, experiment with the following:

- With palms facing up, we accumulate energy in our bodies.
- With palms facing down, we discharge energy.
- Closing all our fingers over our thumbs, when our thumbs are held across our palms, helps to retain energy by stopping its flow from our hands.
- Putting our hands on our bodies energises us in those areas.
- Having our hands in the air around our bodies energises our auras in those areas.
- Placing a hand anywhere on our bodies creates a circuit through which energy flows in both directions.
- Holding our palms and fingers together in front of our bodies with the fingers facing up (the 'Christian' prayer position) balances our systems laterally and vertically, and energises the body particularly at the height of the palms.

Exercise 2: Experimenting with Mudras. Experiment for yourself and discover from your own experience what effect your hands produce. Each position has its advantages and pleasures. Try anything that occurs to you. Enjoy exploring and log your results.

MOVING AND MEDITATION

Regular movement during meditation is recommended. It can make your meditations much more comfortable and maximise the results you get. It helps your body remain open, keeps your energies free and flowing, and helps you stay alert and aware. It also enables you to meditate comfortably for longer periods than if you stay still.

By contrast, though sustained stillness during meditation tends to increase congestion and contractedness, it is recommended by some teachers as being essential in meditation. The difficulty with this advice is that many people are physically and temperamentally unsuited to stillness, particularly in the early stages of learning to meditate. To expect them to stay still is to expect a virtual impossibility, and their efforts to comply can create major obstacles to their practices. At the same time, stillness does have a place for people inclined to fidget or agitate because the stillness helps them to settle inside.

Moving Deliberately During Meditation

Whatever posture you adopt, movement will help your meditation. The best results come from moving so that you stretch and mobilise specific parts of your body in relation to other parts; for example, rotating your shoulders, twisting your spine first one way and then the other, moving your chest in relation to your belly, stretching and flexing your legs and rocking your hips and buttocks back and forth. When sitting, you can also rock your torso back and forth, or from side to side.

Moving at least a little every three to five minutes is helpful during the early years of your practice. This need gradually decreases with the passage of time until you can eventually stay both still and remain open for extended periods.

If you favour staying completely still, then you need to take regular breaks. This approach involves interrupting your meditations by standing up, moving around for at least five minutes, while mobilising different parts of your body in relation to each other, and concentrating on grounding. Then you go back into your meditations. You would take these breaks from complete stillness at least once every 15 to 20 minutes in the early years.

Spontaneous Movement

Our bodies will often move spontaneously while we meditate.

These movements are to do with our muscles, tendons and joints adjusting of their own accord to the energy flowing through them, which is a good thing. Called *kriyas*, they are well known in many yoga circles. When open and flexible enough, our systems accommodate to the flow of energy without movement. However, when they are not open enough, *kriyas* encourage the energy to move through us. The possibilities include: localised vibrating or twitching in muscles, vigorous contraction and relaxation of major muscle groups, arms floating up in the air or waving around, rocking, rotating or shaking of the upper body, and soft to loud sounds, some coming gently, some erupting.

We can generally stop a kriya if we need to. It is our acceptance that allows *kriyas* to proceed. And generally this is a good thing because what is happening is actually clearing and releasing our bodies – awakening our consciousness – and reducing the intensity of future movements.

Interfering with Meditation

Kriyas are a wonderful bonus and well worth any temporary interruption they may cause. Contrary to our subjective experience at times, however; when we move, whether spontaneously or not, we are not interrupting our awakening, only a temporarily enjoyable experience. In fact, the movements are expanding our capacities to remain open to the experiences we like for longer, by helping to release our contractedness. It is our experience of the 'silt' (old feelings, thoughts, memories, etc) dislodged by the movements that is responsible for the apparent interruptions. Moving helps this release and so makes us clearer.

The Best Thing to Do

Relaxing and enjoying the ride is usually best. As we move spontaneously, we are opening to our life energy. Nevertheless, we need to act sensibly. If you start to have vigorous *kriyas*, you are wise to prepare the area in which you meditate: make sure you have enough space to wave your arms, to swing your body, or to allow whatever you find your body doing. (Seek expert advice if you are concerned about what is happening.)

THE USE OF MUSIC

Where movement is a form of internal stimulation, music gives us external stimulation, which we can use deliberately to enhance our meditations in a variety of ways. Music can give a focus for your attention and help to filter the effects of external distractions. Also, you can hang the mantra on any regular beat you can hear.

Choose music according to the effects that you want to produce. The sound of music stimulates the body as well as the ears. So notice the effects in you and select accordingly.

Music can help to stir up discomfort, which can help clear your system. When listening to music, there are advantages to the discomfort you experience as your contractedness is challenged. This gives you the opportunity to digest what your body is holding.

Regularly changing the music when you meditate is useful. We can easily get into ruts if we stick to one piece or style of music for too long. Our systems have a remarkable capacity to adapt to anything regular (see Chapter 4), which can inhibit our progress.

Avoid Music with Vocals

Whatever your preferences, avoiding music with vocals is a good idea. When we meditate, we are very open and suggestible. In this state, we can unconsciously absorb the literal meaning of any words accompanying the music we use and make them part of our personalities. Given the vocals of many songs, this is not a good idea.

Meditate without Music too

Music itself has programming effects on us, so it is good to do without it at times. The rhythms and melodies of the music you play will lay down similar rhythms and melodies inside you, which can produce patterned limitations in your responses.

Meditating in silence is very powerful. Its power is in the way it encourages us to experience our own processes without the guiding or gilding influence of an external source. Particularly for alignment with I-Am and presence with the Infinite, you need to take opportunities to explore yourself 'in the raw'. To do this, it helps to suspend your worldly fixations and pay attention to your own processes without props or distractions, perhaps to use the *Awakening Meditation* to facilitate this (see Chapter 30). As you do, your eternal nature is revealed instead of remaining submerged by the programs that your music or other practices have offered.

THE VALUE OF EXERCISE

Exercise makes a major contribution to meditation. As witness to this, think of the part exercise has long played in association with it: hatha yoga, tai chi, kum nye, qigong and others. Through their physical impact, such practices will help to strengthen, open and release the body so your consciousness is clear and alive.

Regular exercise stimulates internal organs by massaging them directly. The muscular expansion and contraction keeps our organs healthier by, at the very least, stimulating circulation.

Exercising regularly helps to release and to integrate the energies that arise from feelings, emotions and thoughts. This will help maintain more emotional and cognitive balance, and a greater sense of emotional wellbeing than you otherwise would have. It also helps release collected energies. Just like sponges collect water and silt, our bodies collect feelings and experiences. Repeated physical exercise programs have the effect of 'squeezing our body sponges' regularly and actively ejecting what they have collected.

Regular exercise helps to produce clear thinking, intellectual poise and release from confusion. It enables us to concentrate for more sustained periods. Our bodies and thinking are so connected that when the body is clear, poised, focused and released, thinking is drawn towards having the same qualities.

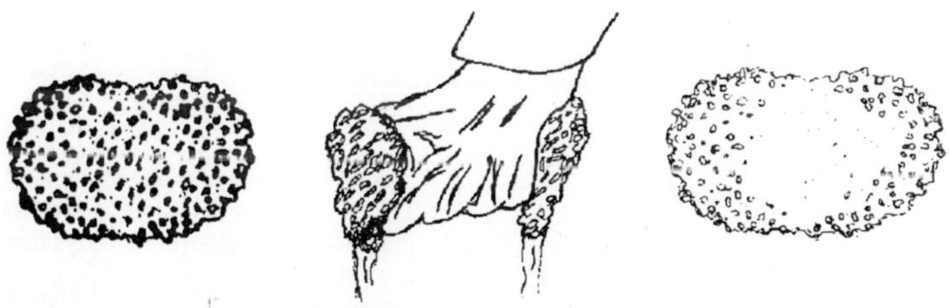

Regular exercise intensifies your physical awareness so all your energies can flow through your body into the physical world. This keeps us open to and flowing with the life energy that is pressing to ground itself through our bodies every moment.

SECTION FIVE
STARTING & PERSISTING

32
STARTING SOMETHING NEW

'Behold the turtle. He makes progress only when he sticks his neck out.'
James Bryant Conant

By this stage, I hope you have found value in what you have read. The suggestions in this book have worked for many people. Of course, while a lot of the techniques will involve doing something new, many require very little extra time from you. In other words, significant changes are possible with minimal effort. Nevertheless:

'To get what you've never had, you must do what you've never done.' Rich Devos
'The doors we open and close each day decide the lives we live.' Flora Whittemore

To help to support your efforts, in this chapter we consider how to make small openings in your life that are big enough for you to start something new. From there, we also consider how to keep expanding what you do a little at a time until you have the full benefits that await your doing so. In fact, devising ways of doing this is a worthwhile priority. After all, what is the good of having a repertoire of effective techniques without using them?

To this end, think of some of what we have already suggested:

- You can do the grounding for a few seconds at a time while doing other things.
- Centring and grounding go together, so you can do both without taking any extra time.
- You can do the relaxation at night when you are already in bed about to go to sleep.
- Thinking about your goals systematically adds little extra to the time you already take. In fact, it may take less.

- 'Living our awareness' is equally undemanding: noticing, accepting and experiencing can accompany everything else we do with just a few 'flicks' of attention to shift emphasis.

All the same, some of the suggestions here do take extra time; time that is, nevertheless, trivial compared with the benefits you can receive. Consider the following examples:

- You can take time to eat breakfast, lunch and your evening meal in balance with your activity levels – and 60% to 95% of all your emotional and psychological problems could dissolve. Do you think these percentages are worthwhile?
- Regularly taking a few minutes to match your short- and medium-term goals with your highest priorities helps to ensure your long-term success. Why waste these opportunities for the want of a few reflective minutes once or twice a week, when these brief periods could mean you become far more successful and more spiritually fulfilled?
- Even taking a few minutes a day to make notes in your logbook, which helps to anchor your learning, may save your life or the quality of your life. Is that worth it to you?

WORKING OUT YOUR STYLE

We each have our own styles of learning and it is worthwhile to discover what they are. The moment we know this, we can devise ways of learning that utilise our natural inclinations. Consider the following examples. While they don't anywhere near exhaust the possibilities, they can prompt you to think about your own style.

Some of us like order and predictability. We enjoy being creatures of habit. We thrive on doing things at the same time and for the same amount of time each day. If this is your preference, make systematic, predictable plans. Of course, other people or events are likely to interfere with your plans at times. A simple solution here is to plan how you will respond to disruptions so you complete what you set out to do as soon as possible after any disruptions occur.

Some of us like spontaneity. We like to do things whenever it occurs to us. We often think of ourselves as free spirits, and prefer to be unbound by anything. We may also feel that planning makes things less significant or less satisfying than what we do on a whim. We find it very challenging when we have to live or work to schedules, meet set requirements or take account of other people's expectations. Planning can seem like confinement, even if we are the ones who have made the plans. Making a general list of your priorities – medium- and long-term – can help. Reviewing your lists spontaneously from time to time can remind you of what is important to you and so keep your priorities alive in your awareness in a way that can also prompt spontaneous action.

Some of us mix spontaneity and predictability. We like doing things spontaneously and in pre-determined ways at times too. In fact, both have advantages and combining approaches is probably what most effective, happy people end up doing. They find ways of organising themselves where they need to and leave space for spontaneity as well. Reaching this balance comes with experience.

Some of us need to align our learning and practices with our 'sensory systems'. If you are visual (a watcher) – you think in pictures, need to see things to understand them, prefer people to be looking at you as you talk, etc – then you are best to devise plans primarily using pictures and in ways that involve your eyes. If you are auditory (a listener) – you hear your thoughts, rely on words for communication, take information in by listening, etc – then you are best to make your plans primarily using sound and in ways that involve your ears. If you are kinaesthetic (a toucher) – you feel your thoughts, rely on physical contact for communication, take information in by getting the feel of what is going on, etc – then you are best to make your plans primarily using touch and physical contact, and in ways that involve the physical use of your body, particularly the skin. If you are olfactory (a smeller) or gustatory (a taster) – you smell and taste your thoughts, rely on fragrances and essences for communication, take information in by smelling and tasting, etc – then you are best to make your plans primarily using smell and taste and to do so in ways that involve your nose and mouth.

Learning can be a far easier task when we align our learning with the natural styles that we use most easily.[49]

Exercise 1: Learning Style. Think about how you learn most easily and enjoyably. How would you describe your style? What works best for you? What works least for you? Make brief notes in your logbook.

STEPS FOR NEW LEARNING

Repetition is an important part of learning. From the moment of our births, we repeat things, often many thousands of times – physical movements, the sounds we make, the patterns in our social contacts; and the ways we communicate, manage our feelings, organise our thinking and control our behaviour. This repetition is needed to program our systems so we can routinely do these things, making it unnecessary for us to relearn something every time we need it. The program is then inside us waiting for our need of it. What we know these days is that the repetitions are actually establishing and strengthening neural pathways – networks of nerves throughout our bodies – that are needed for these functions. The same applies to reprogramming.

I was exposed to our capacity for reprogramming in the early 1970s.[50] Children with speech and reading problems, and people recovering from strokes and brain damage, were put on regimes designed to reprogram the neurological networks used for managing bodily movement, eye-hand coordination, the location of a sound sources in space, speaking, reading and a variety of other things. While the claims of success were doubted at the time, I was excited by the immense potential they offered. In particular, as a psychotherapist, I discovered their broader and successful application with people with psychiatric disorders.

We now have the technology to observe brain functioning and brain changes, both in real time and in static images. Recent work confirms that the principles of programming and reprogramming used by the early pioneers were true. Now called 'neuroplasticity', the capacity for our neurological systems to be reprogrammed and to reprogram themselves is amazing and increasingly accepted.[51,52]

Interestingly, the guidelines for producing effective change discovered by others in their work and by me in my psychotherapeutic work are also now supported by the new research. Five steps usually work best:

1. Identify the current pattern.
2. Identify a desirable new pattern.
3. Interrupt the current pattern.
4. Use the new pattern repeatedly.
5. Start within existing capacities and expand from there.

Step 1: Identify the current pattern. We need to know what we are doing that isn't helpful. Knowing this focuses our attention on what we need to change. As we pay attention to – notice, accept and experience – what is involved, we remain alert to what we are dealing with (see Chapter 13). With nutrition, for example, it helps to know that only eating one major meal at the end of the day is unbalanced and can lead to emotional and psychological problems, not to mention physical imbalances.

Step 2: Identify a desirable new pattern. We need to do something to replace the old pattern. Simply stopping what we are already doing is rarely sufficient, because the old pattern is still inside us and primed to run. What works is to choose to do something deliberately that replaces what is there. By the way, the most efficient way of interrupting an old pattern is to choose something new that is incompatible with our old patterns. Then instead of taking two steps – interrupting the old pattern and starting a new one – we only need concentrate on the new one.

Remember, too, that we need to build up the momentum of the new one so it is at least as strong as the momentum of the one we are replacing. For example, we need to establish a regime of eating three meals a day (and possibly two snacks) that balances with our daily requirements and with our activities at different times of the day and night.

Step 3: Interrupt the current pattern. Clearly this goes hand-in-hand with the last step. Every repetition of the old pattern strengthens our already well-established habits, including the neurological structures and processes that make them possible. It also adds more momentum to the established pattern. Interrupting what we are doing starts both to change us and to reduce the momentum of our old ways.

In fact, old patterns have to be interrupted or their established momentum will keep them rolling on automatically. It is not sufficient simply to notice our unbalanced eating habits, for example. Many people do this for years without changing them. What we need to do is to make a deliberate decision that we will change them – and act on it (see Chapter 24). For example, we start eating at times of the day that we once didn't; or we eat differently, say, more in the morning and less in the evening.

Step 4: Enact the new pattern repeatedly. Using the new pattern becomes our goal (see Chapters 5 to 7). Infrequent repetition, particularly in the early stages, is not sufficient, although it is better than nothing. Only regular, frequent use of the new pattern gets us well accustomed to our new way of eating and to the adjustments we need in relation to food preparation, etc. It also makes the new pattern increasingly automatic as our new activities build their momentum in our systems. In part, this is because the repetition of the new helps to establish alternate neural pathways and to strengthen them. Eventually we will do it all without the need to guard ourselves to ensure that we do. For example, we will keep eating a balanced three meals and two snacks every day for the rest of our lives.

Step 5: Start with existing capacities and expand from there. Instead of trying to achieve everything new from the very beginning, a gradual approach is usually more effective. For example, some people went from no breakfast except thin toast and coffee, to a breakfast of cereal, a thick steak with eggs, and coffee. They understandably found this far too much for their bodies to manage and wanted to stop. We suggested they start with having a liquid breakfast (for example, a lassi or smoothie, soup, congee, eggnog, or egg cream) with their toast, and make a gradual transition to a more substantial breakfast. This worked. By building up slowly, we give ourselves more opportunity to adjust our programs and our bodies. The important thing is, of course, to keep modifying what we do until we have fully changed our patterns to what is required.

Patience is important throughout. Our oldest patterns have many layers of learning on top of them. These take time to change. Proceeding deliberately and persistently is best. So, if you forget or deliberately do something else at times, notice what you have done and get back to your new pattern. Remember to reward yourself for your successes as well, and share your successes with loved ones or others. The sharing is a good way of intensifying the benefits.

Finally, the benefits you get from the changes you make quickly become your reward. You will want to continue! Note that the five steps can be applied to all new learning.

Exercise 2: Replacing Old Patterns. Choose something simple; for example, stopping for five seconds at a time to feel your feet on the ground and to look at, listen to, touch, taste or smell what is around you. This practice only takes a few seconds. Use the steps just outlined to create a simple, achievable program for doing this. Make sure that you decide how many times a day you will do the program; decide how you will remind yourself to do it; and finally, decide deliberately and specifically that you will follow through on your decisions until you are doing everything automatically. Then, just do it! Record the results you get in your logbook.

33
Practising No Matter What

In this moment, and each day of your life from now on, you are faced with a decision, a decision that only you can make. If you are not already using what could improve your life, the decision you face is whether or not you will start doing what is necessary now. If you have started already, your decision is whether or not you will continue. So, what are you going to do?

Exercise 1: Life-Changing Decision. Open your logbook and write: 'From now on in my life I am doing (will do) everything I can to support and expand my personal wellbeing.' After writing this, consider what you have written briefly, maybe by meditating on it for a minute or two and observing your responses as you do. Remember to get yourself grounded and centred too. Record your responses in your logbook, then repeat the statement several times. You could do this exercise regularly every day!

Generally speaking, you have cause for great optimism. Many thousands of people have learnt the lessons in this book. A compendium of commonsense, the suggestions have been discovered and rediscovered for thousands of years. When you learn them, you will not be the first; you won't be the last, either; and the reason for this long history is that the suggestions work. If they didn't, people would not have kept discovering and using them. We can all take heart from this.

Exercise 2: Life Goal. Repeat the following goal several times, aloud if appropriate: 'I am living a happy and fulfilled life; and I remain optimistic and confident that I will continue to do so.' Note your responses in your logbook then repeat the process several more times. This could become a daily mantra for you! Remember that stating a goal like this promotes its completion. It doesn't require that it is already complete.

Now, while decisions to take care of ourselves may seem obvious and attractive, lots of people are not enthusiastic about learning new ways of living or about continuing to use them once they have. There are as many reasons for this as there are people giving them. They say things like:

> *'I would love to learn. I'm sure I'd benefit. But I'm not organised enough.'*
>
> *'Every time I make a start, something happens to distract me. The children, the boss, my clients, or my partner want something from me.'*
>
> *'I got started once and used the practices – for years – then I stopped. I don't really know why any more. I remember they made a difference though.'*
>
> *'I often think about doing one of the practices, but don't seem to get around to it. It just slips my mind and I don't think of it any more until later.'*

DELIBERATE DECISIONS

Deliberate decisions play a crucial part in our success. We discussed this in relation to goal-setting (Chapters 5 to 7) and effective decision-making (Chapter 24). They are important, because whatever energy you have right now for making changes could easily remain free-floating: unfocussed and without a theme. Only definite decisions will give this energy shape and channel it into committed action.

Motivations based on wanting, liking, needing, craving, yearning, hoping, ought-ing, should-ing, must-ing, having to, and the like, involve powerful energies while they are active. We may even feel they will carry us through so that we finally do something based on them. Unfortunately, feeling-based motivations are often inconsistent and rarely last.

For example, tonight we can feel: *'I really want to learn something new', 'I must do my new practice or I'll just keep having all these problems' or 'I know I have to do it – I can't go on like this.'* But tomorrow morning when we wake up we want to stay in bed, or we feel better, or at least better enough not to do anything different, or people distract us from last night's feelings with demands that, yet again, seem to thwart our good intentions.

Definite Decisions

The key is to make a definite decision to do the new practice or exercise. It could be something like: 'I will do ... from now on.'

The important ingredients in this are the commitment, how specific it is, and how deliberate we are as we make the decision. These elements are what get us to act.

Committing ourselves does make a difference. Our commitments link our energies to outcomes and channel those energies into definite courses of action. We no longer leave our behaviour up to our whim in each moment; and we do what we need to do.

These decisions help in another way too. If we start to waver about doing something, the definite nature of our decision helps us to deal actively with our change of mood. Let's say we've made a definite decision to centre ourselves regularly and we are on the verge of not following through. To avoid our commitment, we first have to undo our original decision. And to undo the decision, we need to act as consciously, as deliberately and as definitely as we did when we first made it. This buys us time. Also, think of this: while contemplating a decision not to follow through, we have a chance to commit even more strongly to our original one.

Exercise 3: Definite Decisions. Take any of the practices in this book that have appealed or made sense to you, maybe drinking more water. Make a definite decision that you will do it at least once today. Keep it simple and preferably choose something you can do immediately. Then do it. For example, have a glass of water. Then, in your logbook, record the difference between making a definite decision to do something simple like this and just drifting into or out of it.

Specific Decisions

Specific decisions help us to clarify our commitments. Making them as specific as we can further strengthens their power. A simple way to do this is to remember to ask: *What? When? Where?* What specifically will I do? When specifically will I do it? Where specifically will we do it? A fully expanded commitment looks and sounds like this:

- *'I will do the Mantra Meditation for at least 15 seconds (what), I will do it before breakfast, lunch and dinner (when), and I will do it wherever I am at the time (where).'*
- *'I will start changing my eating and drinking habits by eating breakfast (what), every morning from now on (when), sitting at the table in the kitchen (where).'*

Exercise 4: What, When and Where Commitment? Think of one simple practice you have read in this book. Make a specific commitment to do this practice at least once, if not regularly. Specify 'what', 'when' and 'where' you will do it. Test if making these kinds of commitments helps you to keep them. Many people have found that they do. Note the results in your logbook.

Necessary Flexibility

Flexibility is important at times. After making a definite and specific decision, if something important occurs we may need to interrupt our plans. Before moving off to deal with other things, however, make another decision about *what, when* and *where* you will do what you currently need to postpone.

- *'I need to interrupt my plan now, but I'll do my practice (what), before starting my lunch (when), sitting in the café I plan to go to (where).'*

Making changes clearly and decisively like this helps us to follow through, to be adaptable, and to take responsibility for our actions. Always remember that the most important aspect of this process is to do what we have decided to do.

REMINDING OURSELVES OF OUR GOALS

Many people have important reasons for introducing new ways of living into their lives, including the need to save their lives, to deal with serious bodily or other conditions, or to resolve extreme emotional, situational or other disturbances. Other reasons are to do with finding fulfilment in life, expanding spirituality, making the most of ourselves, and with making life easier. Whatever our reasons, they have their own validity and their own motivating power.

As mentioned, our commitments help to ensure that we achieve our goals by harnessing the energy of our motivations. If we start to waver in our commitments, a powerful way of renewing them is to review our goals and priorities (see Chapters 6 and 7). The moment we do this, we re-stimulate the motivating power of those goals. Of course, as ever, we then need to recommit and to act on our decisions.

34
FINDING GOOD TEACHERS, MASTERS & MENTORS

Because much of our learning is done through interaction with people and the world around us, others have contributed to almost every area of our lives. A great help at times and often a necessity, the knowledge, talents and experience people can offer us can be invaluable. Of course, making this point doesn't diminish the importance of our own efforts, nor of the value of books and other teaching aids.

DIFFERENT TYPES OF GUIDES

In this chapter, we consider three different kinds of guides: teachers, masters and mentors. We also discuss how to get the most from our contacts with each of them.

Definition: Teachers are people who can instruct us about a subject or set of practices.

Teachers don't need to have had direct experience of the subjects they teach, although they may have. Teachers may teach, for example, from what they have read, the verbal reports of others, what they have seen in the media, or what they make up for themselves. Many people who teach meditation and life skills are teachers in this sense.

Definition: Masters are people who have mastered what they teach through directly experiencing and becoming proficient with it.

Masters are skilled enough in the areas of their mastery to manage what is involved so routinely that they don't need to think about it any longer. They live the subjects and the practices they teach. Unlike those teachers who are not masters, the understanding and skill of masters comes from their own experience. In other words, they know what they teach because they are what they teach and are proficient in the practices associated with it (see Chapters 2 and 12). They may well have learned about the areas they have mastered, too; however, their teaching is based on direct experience, not just on imbibing information. While not all masters teach meditation or life skill practices, many do.

Definition: Mentors are masters who deliberately engage with their students to prompt them to deal with relevant personal issues associated with their learning.

Mentors do this through personal encounters, interaction and involvement. Mentors and their trainees often share a commitment to each other. They count on a level of availability that will enable them to complete the emotional and other processes associated with the teaching/learning in which they are mutually engaged. Mentors use their relationships with their trainees as instruments for promoting progress. Generally, it is assumed here and asserted that a mentor has mastered the practices and other aspects of his or her repertoire. (This is a different expectation from popular uses of the word these days.) Many spiritual mentors teach meditation and everyday living skills and practices. although not all do.

WAYS IN WHICH GUIDES CAN HELP

All three can assist our progress in their own ways. Using a 'breathing meditation' as an example, their distinctive contributions could be as follows:

If we need information, teachers are equipped to help us. Also, when we don't know what to do, teachers may help by telling us about something that others have done.

The teacher teaches us: 'There are special breathing meditations that help people to build up life force in their bodies. These meditations are part of a discipline called *pranayama.* I suggest that you try this one (specifies it). I've heard that it's good.'

If we need experience and expertise, masters are the ones to consult. A teacher's helpfulness tends to reach its limits when we need someone's direct experience to help us to take our next steps.

The master offers us: 'To get the best results, you need to change the way you're doing this breathing meditation. How you're doing it is now holding you back. Try doing (specifies something) at the end of the out-breath and doing (specifies something else) at the end of the in-breath. These changes will pave the way for another step. When you've mastered what I've just suggested, I'll take you on further. You'll be ready then.'

If we need close involvement to help us to change personally, we need to find mentors. As our meditation and other practices unfold, we will inevitably have to deal with personal issues. Having people with the necessary skill and experience who are willing to engage with us to help us to resolve our issues is often helpful.

The mentor engages us: You become aware that you have stopped your daily routine and are very caught up in your resistance to your practice. Also noticing this, your mentor says, 'Your breathing meditations have helped you to achieve much. Yet you've stopped doing them, even knowing that they help. You told me that you'd do them daily. Why, when you made that commitment, are you not keeping it?' There follows a direct exchange that helps to deal with your personal reluctance. These exchanges continue through the days and weeks that follow, until you are fully resolved. When resolved, you have developed the capacity to decide to do things that are good for you and to follow through and do them, even if other things create distractions. Mentors may also teach meditation, although, again, not all do.

Clearly, one person may act as a teacher in some areas, a master in some areas and a mentor in others.

COMPETENCE

We have some remarkable people available to us these days. Many of them offer wonderful guidance and help to us. Unfortunately, not all teachers, masters and mentors are equally competent, experienced or caring.[53, 54] We need to take this into account as we approach people whom we hope will help us with our spiritual and life skills practices. The following guidelines are offered to help with this.

1. Keep taking responsibility for yourself. Whomever you approach, you need to remember that you are responsible. Only you are living your life. No one else is. Be aware that some guides invite people into unhelpfully dependent relationships. They try to take their trainees' power into themselves, power that should remain with the trainees. Alternatively, many guides accept or don't stop the attempts of trainees to get them to take over. This is not helpful either.

2. Get the facts. It is wise to gather information about the people you wish to approach. Talk to others, if they are available. Do a search on the Internet. You can also visit potential guides and find out for yourself what they are like. Satisfy yourself that they know what they are doing and, as people, are good for you. Taking great care is warranted when you are thinking of trusting others for help with your life.

3. *Test every statement, assertion, implication or lesson.* In some ways it is natural to accept uncritically what experts or so-called experts suggest. However, this is not a good idea. Some people seem wonderfully confident as they teach things that are false or unreal. So avoid relying on other people's learning, even if they seem knowledgeable, charismatic or would give you a hard time if you disagree with them. You need to test and keep testing everything for yourself.

4. *Only accept as true what you have discovered for yourself is true.* The idea of this is for you to take a stand on what you know from your own experience. When you discover the truth of something, it is good to accept its truth yourself and perhaps to assert it to others. Until you have confirmed for yourself that something is true, however, you are wise to avoid acting as if you know that it is. As with what is true, if you confirm that something is false, then you are wise to acknowledge this, at least to yourself, even if others disagree with you. Staying open to changing your views with further experience is an important part of this orientation, and offers protection from becoming rigid about your past experiences or closed to new ones.

5. *If you find your contact with your guide is working well for you then stay and enjoy the benefits.* Celebrate the opportunities offered and get the most out of them.

6. *If you find your contact is not working well for you in any way, re-evaluate what you are doing.* First, you can talk to your guides about anything troubling you; then if you cannot resolve it and it is a serious issue, you are wise to move on. Leaving a situation is best if you are at risk physically, emotionally or mentally. There is little virtue in staying around for a long time in the futile hope that your guides will change. There are almost certainly other people available who could assist you.

7. *Of course, apply all these guidelines to everything you read in this book, including these guidelines themselves!*

SPECIAL EFFECTS

Masters or mentors can make distinctive contributions that others cannot. Their realised personal capacities rub off on us, just by our spending time with them. Their brilliance brightens ours, their vibrancy intensifies ours, their quietness deepens ours, and their sweetness heightens ours. These people are helpful and powerful catalysts when we want to realise similar qualities and processes for ourselves.

Simply being with them can initiate us directly into the processes that they have already mastered. Their imprint makes our learning easier (see Chapter 29). Teachers cannot do this kind of thing because they only know about the subjects they teach. This contrast between teachers and others is quickly obvious when we meet a master of something. Masters and mentors are also capable of various forms of direct transmission through their mastery – often a wonderful experience, and a great time-saver.

MORE THAN ONE GUIDE

In the past, the guides and devotees of many systems taught that their approaches and leaders were the only ones that were worthwhile – the only real ones. All others were lacking in some way, or were fakes. This limited people's options enormously.

Some people also taught that dire consequences would flow to the meditation practitioner or life-skill trainee who went to other people. Their trainees were told that they had to stick to what they had and not venture elsewhere. Lots of pressure, sometimes abusively, was applied to people to get them to adhere to these expectations.

Nowadays, things have changed considerably. Boundaries between systems are dissolving. People are also increasingly encouraged to seek out others so they can broaden their exposure and enrich their practices. This is a great improvement. We can benefit from many different people. For example, during some periods as we evolve spiritually, or when faced with special challenges, certain guides may be able to help us much better than others.

Also, because effective practice results in change, we may sometimes need to go elsewhere to get what we require for our next steps. At the same time, before leaving, it is worthwhile testing if our current guides do have the mastery we now need. They may not have noticed what we need, for example, and checking will alert them. However, if in the end our guides demonstrate that they don't have what we need, we are wise to go. There is no fault in this, whatever others may say.

At the same time, the way we move on is important. It is best to make these kinds of changes inclusively, to practise goodwill and ongoing appreciation of our past guides. It is also important that we continue to honour all their contributions and to avoid acting as if something is wrong with those we have left behind. These people have had a significant impact on our lives. So, as we move on, we need to remain open to returning, whether to share our recent activities or simply to catch up with them.

Exercise 1: Teachers, Masters and Mentors. Think about people who have been involved in your learning. Using the definitions given above, identify at least one person whom you know was a teacher, one who was a master, and one who was a mentor. They may be people who have guided you, or they could have been associated with others. Record their names and the main qualities you associate with them in your logbook.

Conclusion: You Matter

Above all else, only do what you are ready to do. Take your time. Give yourself the chance to learn. You can and will learn by persisting. Look at, listen to, feel for, and talk to yourself about what is important to you in your life. Once discovered, decide to follow through and affirm, 'I am doing this, because I am worth it.'

References

1. *The Higher Pantheism*, Alfred Lord Tennyson, 1869.
2. Pearsall Professor Paul, *The Heart's Code: Tapping the Wisdom and Power of Our Heart Energy*, Broadway Books, NY, 1998.
3. Kornfield Jack, *A Path with Heart: A guide through the perils and promises of spiritual life*, Bantam Books, NY, 1993.
4. McTaggart Lynne, *The Field*, Element, London, 2001.
5. McTaggart Lynne, *The Intention Experiment: Using Your Thoughts to Change Your Life and the World*, Free Press, London, 2007.
6. Doidge Norman MD, *The Brain that Changes Itself: Stories of personal triumph from the frontiers of brain science*, Scribe Publications, North Carlton, Victoria, Australia, 2010.
7. The meditation is an adaptation of the yoga practice known as *Samyama*. See: Taimni I.K., *The Science of Yoga*, The Theosophical Publishing House, India, 1961, pp286–7.
8. You can use the *Relaxation Meditation* (The Awakening Network Inc., Seymour, Australia). It produces profoundly relaxed states.
9. Shapiro Shauna L., Walsh Roger, & Britton Willoughby B., An Analysis of Recent Meditation Research and Suggestions for Future Directions', *Journal for Meditation and Meditation Research*, 2003, Vol. 3, pp69–90.
10. Maharishi Vedic University, *Scientific Research on Maharishi's Transcendental Meditation and TM-Sidhi Program: A Review*, Cambridge, MA, USA.
11. Murphy Michael, & Donovan Steven, *The Physical and Psychological Effects of Meditation: A Review of Contemporary Research with a Comprehensive Bibliography 1931–1996*, 2nd Edition, Institute of Noetic Science, Sausalito, CA, USA, 1997.
12. Mellor Ken, *Complete Health Meditation*, The Awakening Network Inc., Seymour, Australia, 1992.
13. Mellor Ken, *Vedic Mantra Meditation*, The Awakening Network Inc., Seymour, Australia, 1992.
14. Mellor Ken, *Grounding Meditation*, The Awakening Network Inc., Seymour, Australia, 1988.

15. Mellor Ken, *Relaxation Meditation*, The Awakening Network Inc., Seymour, Australia, 1985.
16. 'Philippians 4:7', *The Holy Bible: Reference Edition*, Thomas Nelson Publishers, Nashville, 1976.
17. Mellor Ken, *Taking Charge: Task Analysis, Option Development, Problem Solving*, PIT Publishing, Melbourne, 1980, p25.
18. Mellor Ken, *Taking Charge: Task Analysis, Option Development, Problem Solving*, PIT Publishing, Melbourne, 1980, Chapter 2, pp23–32.
19. Mellor Ken, *Creative Release Meditation*, The Awakening Network Inc., Seymour, Australia, 1986. This meditation teaches simple steps for setting goals. The recording also includes an extensive introduction that expands what you have read here.
20. Not a direct quote, this story is told in Covey Stephen R. and Merrill Roger A., *First Things First*, Simon and Schuster, UK, 2003.
21. A more detailed description of how to divide tasks/goals into sub-tasks/sub-goals is in Mellor Ken, Chapter 4: *Subtasks and Roles, Taking Charge: Task Analysis, Option Development, Problem Solving*, PIT Publishing, Melbourne, 1980, pp41–51.
22. *Grounding* is, in some ways, very similar to practising *mindfulness*, although I evolved this approach in the early 1980s as part of my psychotherapy work, not from within my meditation practice.
23. Mellor Ken, *Grounding Meditation*, The Awakening Network Inc., Seymour, Australia, 1988.
24. Mellor Ken, *Grounding Meditation*, The Awakening Network Inc., Seymour, Australia, 1988.
25. In some cultures there is little understanding of 'me', 'I' or I-Am'. Identity is derived from our place in our families or the community, and notions of individuality outside those norms are not fostered and may not be understood. I know little about the implications of this sort of background to centring as I have described it.
26. Two recorded meditations are available for learning this: Mellor Ken, *Centering Meditation* and Mellor Ken, *Grounding Meditation* (Both from The Awakening Network Inc., Seymour, Australia, 1988.)
27. This was not formal research. We kept notes about our findings, but did no statistical analysis. Nevertheless, the

patterns were so strikingly obvious that there was no doubt about them: there were obvious links between eating and wellbeing, and between eating and problem resolution.

28. Campbell Colin T. & Campbell Thomas M., *The China Study: Startling Implications for Diet, Weight Loss and Long-term Health*, BenBella Books Inc., Dallas, Texas, USA, 2006.
29. Plant, Professor Jane: *Your Life in Your Hands*, Thomas Dunn Books, NY, USA, 2001.
30. Jelinek Professor George, *Taking Control of Multiple Sclerosis: Natural and Medical Therapies to Prevent its Progression*, Hyland House Publishing, Melbourne, Australia, 2005.
31. Gillespie David, *Sweet Poison: Why Sugar Makes Us Fat*, Viking, Penguin Group, Australia, 2008.
32. This could partly explain why people use food for comfort; although this would clearly only be one element amongst an often complex set of factors that contribute to over eating.
33. Pitchford Paul, *Healing with Whole Foods: Oriental Traditions and Modern Nutrition*, North Atlantic Books, Berkeley, CA, USA, 1993.
34. Mellor Ken, *Creative Release Meditation*, The Awakening Network Inc., Seymour, Australia, 1986.
35. Mellor Ken, *Relaxation Meditation*, The Awakening Network Inc., Seymour, Australia, 1988.
36. Mellor Ken, *Grounding Meditation*, The Awakening Network Inc., Seymour, Australia, 1988.
37. The ways people respond to their own and other people's feelings vary from culture to culture. For example, we can be anything from very demonstrative to very self-contained. There is no right way to do this, so be relaxed about what you are reading and use it as a prompt for you to think about how you and others around you respond.
38. Mellor Ken, *Unifying Meditation*, The Awakening Network Inc., Seymour, Australia, 1988.
39. The *Unifying Meditation* is effective with many different kinds of conflicts. In this chapter, the discussion is mainly confined to conflict between two people.
40. Mellor Ken, *Taking Charge: Task Analysis, Option Development, Problem Solving*, PIT Publishing, Melbourne, 1980, pp94–102.
41. Welch Suzy: *10-10-10: 10 Minutes, 10 Months, 10 Years – A Life-Transforming Idea*, Scribner, NY, USA, 2009.
42. I highly recommend that you buy her book and benefit from

her expertise and the richness of her many examples of how we can apply her system in our lives.

43. *Pranayama Yoga* is the ancient science of breath control and the mobilising of life energy. It is also used to promote awakening and entering *Samadhi*, a transcendent state of consciousness.
44. See also: Mellor Ken, *Purifying Meditation: Alive Breathing, Lotus Breathing* and *Fire Body Meditations*, The Awakening Network Inc., Seymour, Australia, 1988, and Mellor Ken, *Sublime Meditation: Spiral Breathing Meditation*, The Awakening Network Inc., Seymour, Australia, 1992.
45. Chia Mantak, Chapter 3, *Awaken Healing Energy Through the Tao*, Aurora Press, Santa Fe, New Mexico, USA, 1983, pp17–28.
46. Mellor Ken and Mellor Elizabeth, *ParentCraft: A practical guide to raising children well,* 2nd Edition, Finch Publishing, Sydney, Australia, 2001, pp74–83.
47. Mellor Ken, *Vedic Mantra Meditation*, The Awakening Network Inc., Seymour, Australia, 1992.
48. The Awakening Network has a *Vedic Mantra Meditation* recording that initiates users and, with repeated use, helps to expand their practice. Elizabeth and I are also available to initiate people in person or at a distance. You will find contact details at the end of the book.
49. This material is drawn from Neuro Linguistic Programming (NLP), an approach to communication, inner processing and more that is worth investigating. See Ready Rimilla and Burton Kate, *Neuro Linguistic Programming for Dummies*, 2011.
50. Delacato Carl H., *A New Start for the Child with Reading Problems*, David McKay Company Inc. NY, USA, 1970.
51. Doidge Norman, *The Brain that Changes Itself: Stories of personal triumph from the frontiers of brain science*, Revised Edition, Scribe, Melbourne, Australia, 2010.
52. Computer programs, therapeutic systems, and electronic games are now being produced for people to improve brain functioning in many different areas.
53. Caplan Marianna, *Halfway Up the Mountain: The Error of Premature Claims to Enlightenment*, Hohm Press, Prescott, AZ, USA, 1999.
54. Caplan Marianna, *Do You Need a Guru? Understanding the student-teacher relationship in an era of false prophets*, Thorsons, London, 2002.

Bibliography

Campbell T. Colin, PhD, and Campbell Thomas M., II, *The China Study: Startling Implications for Diet, Weight Loss and Long-term Health*, BenBella Books Inc., Dallas, 2006.

Caplan Marianna, *Halfway Up the Mountain: The Error of Premature Claims to Enlightenment*, Hohm Press, Prescott, AZ, USA, 1999.

Caplan Marianna, *Do You Need a Guru? Understanding the student-teacher relationship in an era of false prophets*, Thorsons, London, 2002.

Chia Mantak, *Awaken Healing Energy Through the Tao*, Aurora Press, Santa Fe, New Mexico, USA, 1983.

Covey Stephen R. and Merrill A. Roger, *First Things First*, Simon and Schuster, U.K., 2003.

Delacato Carl H., *A New Start for the Child with Reading Problems*, David McKay Company Inc. NY, USA, 1970.

Doidge Norman, MD, *The Brain the Changes Itself: Stories of personal triumph from the frontiers of brain science*, Revised Edition, Scribe Publications, Melbourne, Australia, 2010.

Gillespie David, *Sweet Poison: Why Sugar Makes Us Fat*, Viking, Penguin Group (Australia), 2008.

Jelinek Professor George, *Taking Control of Multiple Sclerosis: Natural and Medical Therapies to Prevent its Progression*, Hyland House Publishing, Melbourne, 2005.

Kornfield Jack, *A Path with Heart: A guide through the perils and promises of spiritual life*, Bantam Books, NY, NY, 1993.

Maharishi Vedic University, *Scientific Research on Maharishi's Transcendental Meditation and TM-Sidhi Program: A Review*, Cambridge, MA, USA.

McTaggart Lynne, *The Field*, Element, London, 2001.

McTaggart Lynne, *The Intention Experiment: Using Your Thoughts to Change Your Life and the* World, Free Press, London, 2007.

Mellor Ken, *Complete Health Meditation*, The Awakening Network Inc., Seymour, Australia, 1992.

Mellor Ken, *Taking Charge: Task Analysis, Option Development, Problem Solving*, PIT Publishing, Melbourne, 1980.

Mellor Ken, *Relaxation Meditation*, The Awakening Network Inc., Seymour, Australia, 1985.

Mellor Ken, *Creative Release Meditation*, The Awakening Network Inc., Seymour, Australia, 1986.

Mellor, Ken *Grounding Meditation*, The Awakening Network Inc., Seymour, Australia, 1988.

Mellor Ken, *Purifying Meditation : Alive Breathing Meditation, Lotus Breathing Meditation* and *Fire Body Meditation*, The Awakening Network Inc., Seymour, Australia, 1988.

Mellor Ken, *Sublime Meditation*: *Spiral Breathing Meditation*, The Awakening Network Inc., Seymour, Australia, 1992.

Mellor Ken, *Vedic Mantra Meditation*, The Awakening Network Inc., Seymour, Australia, 1992.

Mellor Ken, *Centering Meditation*, The Awakening Network Inc., Seymour, Australia, 2002.

Mellor Ken and Mellor Elizabeth, *ParentCraft: A practical guide to raising children well,* 2nd Ed, Finch Publishing, Sydney, Australia, 2001.

Murphy Michael, and Donovan Steven, *The Physical and Psychological Effects of Meditation: A review of Contemporary Research with a Comprehensive Bibliography 1931 – 1996*, 2nd Edition, Institute of Noetic Science, Sausalito, CA, 1997.

Pearsall Professor Paul, *The Heart's Code: Tapping the Wisdom and Power of Our Heart* Energy, Broadway Books, NY, NY, 1998.

Philippians 4:7, *The Holy Bible: Reference Edition*, Thomas Nelson Publishers, Nashville, 1976.

Pitchford Paul, *Healing with Whole Foods: Oriental Traditions and Modern Nutrition*. North Atlantic Books, Berkeley, CA, USA, 1993.

Plant, Professor Jane: *Your Life in Your Hands*, Thomas Dunn Books, NY, NY, 2001.

Shapiro Shauna L., Walsh Roger, & Britton Willoughby B., *An Analysis of Recent Meditation Research and Suggestions for Future Directions*, Journal for Meditation and Meditation Research, 2003, Vol. 3, pp.69–90.

Taimni I.K., *The Science of Yoga*, The Theosophical Publishing House, India, 1961.

Tennyson Alfred Lord, *The Higher Pantheism*, 1869.

Welch Suzy: *10-10-10: 10 Minutes, 10 Months, 10 Years – A Life-Transforming Idea* (Scribner, NY, NY, USA 2009.)

Index